Mormon Mama

ITALIAN COOKBOOK

FROM MY NONA ROSA'S TABLE TO YOURS

Mormon Mama
ITALIAN COOKBOOK

FROM MY NONA ROSA'S TABLE TO YOURS

SHANNON M. SMURTHWAITE

FRONT TABLE BOOKS
AN IMPRINT OF CEDAR FORT, INC.
SPRINGVILLE, UTAH

ISBN: 978-1-4621-1109-1

Published by Front Table Books, an imprint of Cedar Fort, Inc., 2373 W. 700 S., Springville, UT 84663
Distributed by Cedar Fort, Inc., www.cedarfort.com

Library of Congress Cataloging-in-Publication data on file

Cover and page design by Angela D. Olsen
Cover design © 2013 by Lyle Mortimer
Edited by Michelle Stoll

Printed in China

10 9 8 7 6 5 4 3 2 1

✳ ✳ ✳ ✳ ✳ ✳ ✳ ✳ ✳ ✳ ✳ ✳ ✳ ✳ ✳ ✳ ✳ ✳ ✳ ✳

DEDICATION

To my mother and grandmother for teaching me. For my daughter, Kelly, who inspired this compilation and blessed it with her own amazing talents. To our other children: Emily, Christopher, and K.C., and my husband, Donald, who put up with my culinary creations (the yummy and not so) through the years. And for dear friends and extended family who kindly shared tried-and-true recipes. Thank you to my editor, Michelle Stoll, for her enthusiasm and appetite for this project.

Thank you to Kelly S. Schumacher and Elise Pessetto Poulson for their wonderful photography work.

Famiglia e amici!

Adams	*Hansen*	*Schumacher*
Barney	*Jannuzzi*	*Shelton*
Cannariato	*Johnson*	*Smith*
Carter	*Margaris*	*Smurthwaite*
Cluff	*Neider*	*Thatcher*
D'Amico	*Pessetto*	*Venezia*
Dispensiero	*Poulson*	*Walter*
Gallinger	*Rosa*	*Zanasi*
Gallo		

✳ ✳ ✳ ✳ ✳ ✳ ✳ ✳ ✳ ✳ ✳ ✳ ✳ ✳ ✳ ✳ ✳ ✳ ✳ ✳

CONTENTS

✳ ✳ ✳ ✳ ✳ ✳ ✳ ✳ ✳ ✳ ✳ ✳ ✳ ✳ ✳ ✳ ✳ ✳

✳ ✳ ✳ ✳ ✳ ✳ ✳ ✳ ✳ ✳ ✳ ✳ ✳ ✳ ✳ ✳ ✳ ✳

CONTENTS

THE INGREDIENTS OF TWO CULTURES

From Author Shannon M. Smurthwaite

✳ ✳ ✳ ✳ ✳ ✳ ✳ ✳ ✳ ✳ ✳ ✳ ✳ ✳ ✳ ✳ ✳ ✳ ✳

MY MOTHER'S FAMILY CAME FROM ITALY. My father's family came from Scotland.

The Rosas left their native land, crossed icy winter oceans, and got their first taste of America at Ellis Island. A few years after marrying, my grandparents and their only child, my mother, left for southern California.

My father's family crossed the rugged plains with early Mormon pioneers and, after a generation or two, also ended up in southern California.

I grew up with a unique blend of traditions and cultures, especially given my mother's conversion to the LDS faith as a young woman. As a full-blooded Italian born of Roman Catholic parents, she brought a special vitality to our family and those who knew her. I had the best of two worlds and two cultures, the prudent Scottish influence of my father's family and the zesty Italian ancestry of my mother. I've been deeply influenced by both sides of my family, and I'm grateful for my rich heritage.

When it came to the kitchen, though, the Italian side of the family reigned. I quickly learned the "dump and taste" method. Very few written recipes were found in my mother's and grandmother's kitchens. If it looked good and tasted right, it was ready to eat. When I asked Nanny, my tiny grandmother from Naples, for her recipes, she always replied, "Oh, doll, it's just a little of this and a little of that."

For years, I have gathered, tasted, tweaked, and simplified Italian family recipes, taking careful notes. I wanted these recipes written down! My hope is to squash the myth that Italian cooking is difficult. Fear not! These pages contain delightful meals—sure to please and comfort, and many of them not requiring as much time and labor as you think. In this collection of truly Italian family recipes, you'll find the entire range, from the super-simple to those requiring a bit more time and effort.

My mother and grandmother have since passed on, but I believe in the power of scent. When preparing their recipes, it quickly takes me back to memories of watching them work their kitchen wizardry. They are with me.

So open the book, select a recipe, gather your family and friends, and begin to make your own memories.

Buon appetito,

Shannon

✳ ✳ ✳ ✳ ✳ ✳ ✳ ✳ ✳ ✳ ✳ ✳ ✳ ✳ ✳ ✳ ✳ ✳ ✳

APPETIZERS
& MORE

I

2

Stuffed Mushrooms

This is a recipe from my good friend (and fellow Italian!) Monica Cannariato-Walter.

Makes
6
Servings

Ingredienti:

1 lb. Italian sausage, cooked and drained

1 bunch green onions (chopped)

1 (8-oz.) pkg. cream cheese, room temperature

30 large mushrooms, washed and stems removed

Parmesan cheese (garnish)

Istruzioni:

Preheat oven to 350 degrees. In a bowl, blend cooked sausage (cooled), green onions, and cream cheese. Stuff mixture carefully in to the cavity of each mushroom. Bake upright for 30 minutes. Sprinkle with Parmesan cheese before serving.

"Chi va a letto senza cena tutta la notte si dimena."
(Translation: He who goes to bed without eating
will regret it throughout the night.)

Italian Nachos

✳ ✳ ✳ ✳ ✳ ✳ ✳ ✳ ✳ ✳ ✳ ✳ ✳ ✳ ✳ ✳ ✳ ✳ ✳ ✳

Makes **4** Servings

Ingredienti:

1½ Tbsp. olive oil

1 package of wonton wrappers (or ½ package of egg roll wrappers), cut in to chip-size strips

12 oz. Italian sausage, browned

18–20 black olives, sliced

½ cup banana peppers

2 Roma tomatoes, chopped

Parmesan cheese

cheddar cheese sauce (recipe on the right)

Istruzioni:

Heat oil in a skillet. Fry wonton (or egg roll) strips in oil until light brown, even just in spots, on each side. Remove from oil and place on paper towels to remove excess oil.

Layer sausage, olives, peppers, and tomatoes over layers of wonton chips. Drizzle cheddar cheese sauce over the top. Sprinkle with Parmesan cheese.

CHEDDAR CHEESE SAUCE

1½ Tbsp. unsalted butter

1½ Tbsp. flour

salt and pepper to taste

¾ cup 2-percent milk

¾ cup medium cheddar cheese, grated

1½ Tbsp. grated Parmesan cheese

Istruzioni:

Melt butter in saucepan. Remove from heat. Stir in flour (with a whisk) to make a roux. Season with salt and pepper. Slowly add milk, stirring constantly and return pan to medium heat. Cook for about 6 minutes (again stirring frequently) until the sauce thickens. Add cheeses and stir until smooth.

✳ ✳ ✳ ✳ ✳ ✳ ✳ ✳ ✳ ✳ ✳ ✳ ✳ ✳ ✳ ✳ ✳ ✳ ✳ ✳

"Chi se move mangia e chi sta fermo secca."
(Translation: He who moves, eats, and he who stands still, dries up.)

4

Kelly's Orzo & Cheddar Balls

✳ ✳ ✳ ✳ ✳ ✳ ✳ ✳ ✳ ✳ ✳ ✳ ✳ ✳ ✳ ✳ ✳ ✳

Makes
4
Servings

Ingredienti:

¾ cup orzo, cooked and drained

1½ cup shredded cheddar cheese

¾ cup Italian bread crumbs

1 large egg, lightly beaten

vegetable oil for frying

Istruzioni:

Mix orzo, cheese, and bread crumbs in a bowl. Add egg and coat well. Roll into golf ball–sized balls. Heat deep fryer to 350 degrees. Fry for 2–4 minutes. (You can also fry balls on stovetop in medium saucepan with oil until golden brown.)

✳ ✳ ✳ ✳ ✳ ✳ ✳ ✳ ✳ ✳ ✳ ✳ ✳ ✳ ✳ ✳ ✳ ✳

A clean kitchen is an uneventful kitchen.

Kelly's Orzo and
Cheddar Balls

Nana's Fried Meatballs

Makes **4–6** *Servings*

Ingredienti:

1 lb. chopped ground beef

2 eggs

1 cup unflavored breadcrumbs, divided

¾ cup grated Parmesan cheese

1 tsp. garlic powder

fresh parsley, chopped

salt and pepper to taste

olive oil

Istruzioni:

Mix together (with your hands, of course!) the following ingredients: meat, eggs, ¾ cup breadcrumbs, cheese, garlic, and parsley. Mixture should be a thick consistency. Sprinkle in a few drops of water. Roll into golf ball–sized shapes. Flatten slightly. Roll in reserved breadcrumbs. Fry in olive oil.

It's not uncommon for an Italian father to own a successful business, but drive a car that is 20 years old.

6

Mozzarella and Sundried Tomato Patties ✳✳✳✳✳✳✳✳

Makes **4** *Patties*

Ingredienti:

1 (8-oz.) ball mozzarella, cut into 8 slices

4 tsp. sundried tomato pesto

2 eggs plus 1 tsp. milk, whisked together in a small bowl

½ cup Italian bread crumbs

oil, for frying

Istruzioni:

In a frying pan, warm oil over medium-low heat. Take one slice of mozzarella and spread 1 teaspoon of sundried tomato pesto in the center of the cheese. Take another slice of mozzarella and cover. Dip in egg/milk mixture, then in bread crumbs.

Fry in oil on both sides until crispy. Repeat with remaining ingredients.

These are great as a side dish or appetizer.

The ultimate satisfaction an Italian Nona can have is to have her family full and happy.

Italian Popcorn

✳ ✳ ✳ ✳ ✳ ✳ ✳ ✳ ✳ ✳ ✳ ✳ ✳ ✳ ✳ ✳ ✳ ✳ ✳ ✳

Makes **4** Servings

Ingredienti:

1 bag unpopped microwave popcorn

nonstick cooking spray

3 Tbsp. grated Parmesan cheese

½ tsp. Italian seasoning, crushed

¼ tsp. red pepper flakes

Istruzioni:

Prepare popcorn according to package directions. Put popcorn in large bowl, removing any un-popped kernels. Spray popcorn with cooking spray. Stir until all kernels are coated with spray. Sprinkle Parmesan, Italian seasoning, and red pepper into bowl and stir. Serve immediately.

✳ ✳ ✳ ✳ ✳ ✳ ✳ ✳ ✳ ✳ ✳ ✳ ✳ ✳ ✳ ✳ ✳ ✳ ✳ ✳

"'Tis an ill cook that cannot lick his own fingers."
—William Shakespeare, from Romeo and Juliet

Italian Popcorn

10

Tomato, Mozzarella & Basil Bruschetta

Makes
4–6
Servings

Ingredienti:

1 (32-oz.) can whole tomatoes, drained

1 cup fresh basil

4 Tbsp. extra-virgin olive oil

6 cloves garlic, peeled, divided

salt and freshly ground pepper to taste

1 large or 2 medium French baguettes, sliced

1½ lbs. fresh mozzarella cheese, sliced

Istruzioni:

Preheat oven to 375 degrees. Chop and mix together tomatoes, basil, olive oil, and 2 cloves garlic until chunky (may use a food processor). Season with salt and pepper.

Toast bread slices until light, golden brown on both sides. Rub remaining garlic on bread slices; cover with a slice of cheese. Return to oven for about 45 seconds, to melt cheese.

Remove from oven and cover each slice with a spoonful of tomato mixture.

"Simplicity is the ultimate sophistication."
—Leonardo da Vinci, Italian Artist and Sculptor

Fresh Apple Parsley Dressing

Makes
6–8
Servings

Ingredienti:

1 apple, peeled, cored, and cut into ¼-inch pieces

2 Tbsp. cider vinegar

1 tsp. hot pepper sauce or Tabasco

1 scallion

¼ cup fresh parsley leaves

¾ tsp. salt

¼ tsp. black pepper

2–3 Tbsp. water

½ cup vegetable oil

2 quarts greens, washed and dried

Istruzioni:

Combine first seven ingredients in blender and pulse, scraping down sides and adding water until very finely chopped. With machine running, gradually add oil, scraping down sides as needed. Serve over greens. Dress with slivered almonds, cranberries, and large curls of Parmesan cheese.

Italian women buy two things in bulk: olive oil and Aqua Net.

Italian Strawberry Lemonade

✳ ✳ ✳ ✳ ✳ ✳ ✳ ✳ ✳ ✳ ✳ ✳ ✳ ✳ ✳ ✳ ✳ ✳ ✳ ✳

Makes **8** Servings

Ingredienti:

8 cups lemonade

8 cups ginger ale

3–4 strawberries, washed and thinly sliced

lemon zest

ice

Istruzioni:

In a pitcher, mix lemonade and ginger ale together. Add strawberries and lemon zest. Pour over ice in tall glasses. Enjoy!

✳ ✳ ✳ ✳ ✳ ✳ ✳ ✳ ✳ ✳ ✳ ✳ ✳ ✳ ✳ ✳ ✳ ✳ ✳ ✳

Italian grandmothers don't have much patience
for unruly children in the kitchen.
My Nona kept me busy (and out of the kitchen)
by having me lick her weekly pile of green stamps.

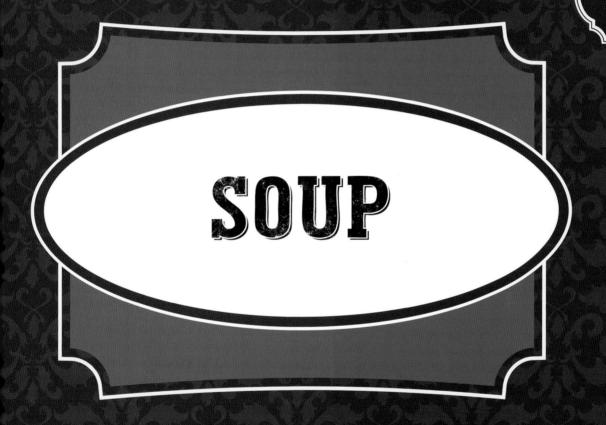

SOUP

Bella Soup

✳ ✳ ✳ ✳ ✳ ✳ ✳ ✳ ✳ ✳ ✳ ✳ ✳ ✳ ✳ ✳ ✳ ✳ ✳ ✳

Makes
4–6
Servings

Ingredienti:

2 Tbsp. butter

1 medium onion chopped

1 clove garlic, finely chopped

1 cup chopped carrots

½ large red pepper, seeded and chopped

32-oz. chicken stock (homemade is preferred)

1 (28-oz.) can whole tomatoes with juice

2 Tbsp. dried basil

2 Tbsp. dried oregano

2 Tbsp. marjoram

2 small bay leaves

sea salt to taste

freshly ground black pepper to taste

½ cup fresh Italian parsley

½ cup fresh baby spinach

1 (15-oz.) can organic kidney beans, drained

8 oz. elbow macaroni

Istruzioni:

Heat a sauté pan over medium heat and add butter. When the butter just begins to bubble, add the onions and sauté until they start to caramelize. Add the garlic, carrots, and red pepper. Let the vegetables continue cooking for about 5 minutes, and then add the broth. Add the crushed tomatoes with the juice. Add the basil, oregano, marjoram, bay leaves, and salt and pepper to taste. Let this simmer for another 5 minutes. Add the parsley, spinach, and beans. Simmer on low for 20–30 minutes.

Meanwhile, cook the pasta according to the directions on the package. Set aside. During the last 5 minutes of soup's cooking time, remove bay leaves and add pasta. This is very yummy, so enjoy!

✳ ✳ ✳ ✳ ✳ ✳ ✳ ✳ ✳ ✳ ✳ ✳ ✳ ✳ ✳ ✳ ✳ ✳ ✳ ✳

Turkey is served on Thanksgiving—*after* the
manicotti, gnocchi, lasagna, and soup.

Chicken Tortellini Soup

Makes **6–8** Servings

Ingredienti:

6–7 cups water

3 (10-oz) cans condensed chicken broth (or use 1 cube chicken bouillon per 1 cup hot water to equal 4 cups—it's less expensive)

1 (10.5-oz) can cream of chicken soup

2 cups cooked chicken, cubed

1 chopped onion

1 cup sliced carrots

2 garlic cloves, minced

½ tsp. dried basil leaves, chopped

½ tsp. dried oregano leaves, chopped

1 (9-oz.) pkg. frozen cut broccoli (I usually just use fresh broccoli)

7 oz. cheese tortellini

grated Parmesan cheese

Istruzioni:

In a large saucepot, combine water, chicken broth, soup, chicken, onions, carrots, garlic, basil, and oregano. Bring to a boil and simmer about an hour. Add tortellini and broccoli. If you use dry tortellini, simmer uncovered for 20 minutes. If you use frozen tortellini, simmer for about 10 minutes, or until done. Serve topped with fresh-grated Parmesan cheese.

Note: I cook the chicken in water in the same pot I am using to make the soup; boil until it is tender. Get rid of the water, break up the chicken, and then make the soup. That way, you don't have to wash two pans!

Never buy grated cheese—always shred the cheese yourself. When cheese is pre-grated, it loses a lot of its flavor.

Mimi's Tomato Soup

✳ ✳ ✳ ✳ ✳ ✳ ✳ ✳ ✳ ✳ ✳ ✳ ✳ ✳ ✳ ✳ ✳ ✳ ✳

Makes
6–8
Servings

Ingredienti & Istruzioni:

In large pot on medium-low heat, sauté:

    1 generous Tbsp. butter.

    1 medium white onion, chopped

Whisk in:

    2–3 Tbsp. flour.

To the above, add:

    2 Tbsp. sugar

    1 Tbsp. salt

Then fold in:

    3 (15-oz.) cans petite-cut, low-sodium tomatoes.

    2–3 cups milk, to the consistency of your liking.

Cook for 15 minutes over medium heat, mixing well. Serve with a crusty loaf of bread.

✳ ✳ ✳ ✳ ✳ ✳ ✳ ✳ ✳ ✳ ✳ ✳ ✳ ✳ ✳ ✳ ✳ ✳ ✳

Italian Proverb:
Friendships and macaroni are best when they are warm.

17

Mimi's
Tomato Soup

Tuscany
Tomato Soup

Tuscany Tomato Soup

Ingredienti:

½ cup olive oil

¼ cup butter

4 carrots, peeled and finely diced

2–3 medium onions, finely minced

4 stalks celery, diced

3 quarts canned tomatoes with juice, or 14 large, ripe fresh tomatoes, peeled and coarsely chopped*

½ cup parsley, finely chopped

6 leaves basil, sliced

salt and pepper to taste

Istruzioni:

Heat oil and butter in heavy kettle. Cook the carrots, onions, and celery for about 20 minutes until tender. Add the tomatoes and continue cooking over moderate heat for another 20–30 minutes. Stir in the parsley and basil. Season with salt and pepper. Simmer a few more minutes. Serve hot.

Include other optional ingredients as you see fit: chopped cabbage, canned white beans, pasta, and so on. Top with a small dollop of sour cream or freshly grated Parmesan cheese when serving.

This soup is great with a green salad or perhaps with a simple grilled cheese sandwich.

*If using the fresh tomatoes instead of canned tomatoes, you will need to add some water.

"Preach the Gospel at all times, and when necessary, use words."
—St. Francis of Assisi

The Best Minestrone Soup

✳ ✳ ✳ ✳ ✳ ✳ ✳ ✳ ✳ ✳ ✳ ✳ ✳ ✳ ✳ ✳ ✳ ✳ ✳

Makes
8
Servings

Ingredienti:

3 Tbsp. olive oil

1 cup white onion, minced
  (about 1 small onion)

¼ cup celery, minced (about ½ stalk)

4 tsp. garlic, minced (about 4 cloves)

½ cup frozen cut Italian green beans

½ cup zucchini, chopped

4 cups vegetable broth (Swanson is good—
  Note: Do not use chicken broth!)

1 (14-oz.) can diced tomatoes, drained

2 (15-oz.) cans red kidney beans, drained

2 (15-oz.) cans small white beans, drained, or
  2 (15-oz.) cans great northern beans, drained

½ cup carrot, julienned or shredded

3 cups hot water

2 Tbsp. minced fresh parsley

1½ tsp. dried oregano

1½ tsp. salt

½ tsp. ground black pepper

½ tsp. dried basil

¼ tsp. dried thyme

4 cups fresh baby spinach

½ cup small shell pasta

Istruzioni:

Heat olive oil over medium heat in a large soup pot. Sauté onion, celery, garlic, green beans, and zucchini in the oil for 5 minutes or until onions begin to turn translucent. Add vegetable broth to pot, plus drained tomatoes, beans, carrot, hot water, and spices. Bring soup to a boil, then reduce heat and allow to simmer for 20 minutes. Add spinach leaves and pasta and cook for an additional 20 minutes, or until desired consistency is reached.

✳ ✳ ✳ ✳ ✳ ✳ ✳ ✳ ✳ ✳ ✳ ✳ ✳ ✳ ✳ ✳ ✳ ✳ ✳

For an Italian mama,
Sunday is not the day of rest, but the day of cooking
for the 18 people she is having over for dinner that evening.

The Best
Minestrone Soup

22

Hearty Italian Soup

✳ ✳ ✳ ✳ ✳ ✳ ✳ ✳ ✳ ✳ ✳ ✳ ✳ ✳ ✳ ✳ ✳ ✳ ✳ ✳

Makes **8** *Servings*

Ingredienti:

2 Tbsp. butter

1 medium onion, chopped

2 cloves garlic, chopped

1 cup chopped carrots

½ large red pepper, seeded and chopped

32 oz. chicken stock

1 (28-oz.) can crushed tomatoes with juice

2 Tbsp. dried basil

2 Tbsp. dried oregano

2 Tbsp. marjoram

2 small bay leaves

sea salt to taste

freshly ground black pepper to taste

½ cup fresh Italian parsley, washed well

½ cup baby spinach, washed well

1 (15-oz.) can kidney beans, drained

8 oz. elbow macaroni

Istruzioni:

Heat butter in pan over medium heat. When butter begins to bubble, add onions and sauté until they caramelize. Add garlic, carrots, and red pepper. Cook vegetables 5 minutes, then add stock. Add tomatoes, with the juice. Add basil, oregano, marjoram, bay leaves, salt, and pepper. Let simmer for another 5 minutes. Add parsley, spinach, and beans. Simmer on low for 30 minutes.

Meanwhile, cook pasta according to package directions. Drain, set aside, and add pasta to soup mixture the last 5 minutes of soup cooking time. Remove bay leaves before serving.

✳ ✳ ✳ ✳ ✳ ✳ ✳ ✳ ✳ ✳ ✳ ✳ ✳ ✳ ✳ ✳ ✳ ✳ ✳ ✳

LDS missionaries from the United States get their hair cut every two weeks. Missionaries from Italy get their hair "oil changed" every two weeks.

BREAD

24

Ciabatta Bread

Ciabatta Bread

✳ ✳

Ingredienti:

1½ cups water

1 tsp. salt (I use fine sea salt)

1 heaping tsp. white sugar

1 Tbsp. olive oil

3¼ cup bread flour

1½ generous tsp. SAF yeast (or any good bread machine yeast)

Makes
1
Loaf

Istruzioni:

In the order above, place ingredients in bread machine. (Yes, yeast goes in last!) Use the "dough" cycle and start. Dough will be sticky when cycle is complete. Fight the urge to add more flour. Place the dough on a lightly floured board and let it rest for 15–20 minutes.

Lightly flour or use parchment-lined baking sheets. (You could sprinkle a little corn meal on the bottom.) Form a flat rectangle with the dough; place dough on a prepared baking sheet. Dimple surface and lightly flour tops. (Dimpling is important, because you want the air bubbles to pop.)

Cover. Let rest 50–90 minutes in a draft-free location. (Rising time varies with altitude, flour type, and so on. I typically allow an hour and fifteen minutes.)

Preheat oven to 425 degrees. After the first rising, dimple dough a second time. Baking times vary depending on your oven, but 22–25 minutes is the suggested duration. Use the middle rack. This is a soft-crust bread.

VARIATIONS:

For a more raised version of this recipe, giving you a taller loaf: Increase sugar to 2 generous teaspoons and increase yeast to 2½ teaspoons. Add 15 minutes to the rising time.

FOR A CHEESIER VERSION: After the bread machine has whirled for ten minutes, open the lid and slowly add 1 generous tablespoon of shredded Romano/Parmesan blend *and* 1 generous tablespoon of shredded mozzarella cheese. *Molto bene!*

NOTE: *This recipe is for a bread machine.*

✳ ✳

Mangia che ti passa
(Translation: Eat and it will be over, you'll feel better.)

26

Rosemary Parmesan Biscuits

Rosemary Parmesan Biscuits

※ ※ ※ ※ ※ ※ ※ ※ ※ ※ ※ ※ ※ ※ ※ ※ ※ ※ ※ ※

Makes **1** *dozen Biscuits*

Ingredienti:

4 cups whole-wheat flour

2 tsp. baking powder

1 tsp. baking soda

½ tsp. salt

½ cup Parmesan cheese

1½ tsp. dry rosemary, crumbled

2 cups milk

3 Tbsp. vegetable oil

Istruzioni:

Mix all dry ingredients. In another bowl, combine milk and oil. Stir both mixtures together. Drop biscuits on lightly greased pan with large spoon. Bake at 425 degrees for 10–12 minutes.

※ ※ ※ ※ ※ ※ ※ ※ ※ ※ ※ ※ ※ ※ ※ ※ ※ ※ ※ ※

Mormon Italian Equivalents:
Coffee = Diet Coke
Wine = Diet Coke
Tea = Diet Coke

Italian Zucchini Bread

✳ ✳ ✳ ✳ ✳ ✳ ✳ ✳ ✳ ✳ ✳ ✳ ✳ ✳ ✳ ✳ ✳ ✳ ✳

Makes
6–8
Servings

Ingredienti:

3 eggs

2 cups sugar

1 cup vegetable oil

2 cups grated, peeled raw zucchini

3 tsp. vanilla extract

3 cups all-purpose flour

1 tsp. salt

1 tsp. baking soda

¼ tsp. double-acting baking powder

3 tsp. ground cinnamon

1 cup chopped walnuts

Istruzioni:

Preheat oven to 350 degrees. Beat eggs until light and foamy. Add sugar, oil, zucchini, and vanilla. Mix gently, but well.

Combine flour, salt, soda, baking powder, and cinnamon and add to egg-zucchini mixture. Stir until well blended. Add nuts and pour into two lightly greased 9x5x3 pans. Bake for 1 hour. Thoroughly cool on rack (about 30 minutes) before slicing.

✳ ✳ ✳ ✳ ✳ ✳ ✳ ✳ ✳ ✳ ✳ ✳ ✳ ✳ ✳ ✳ ✳ ✳ ✳

Every "authentic" Italian meal includes multiple
bottles of 7Up and antacid on the table.

Italian Zucchini Bread

The Best Focaccia Bread Ever

The Best Focaccia Bread Ever

✳ ✳ ✳ ✳ ✳ ✳ ✳ ✳ ✳ ✳ ✳ ✳ ✳ ✳ ✳ ✳ ✳ ✳ ✳ ✳

Ingredienti:

1 heaping Tbsp. sugar

2¼ tsp. yeast (I use SAF)

1¼ cups water, lukewarm from tap

¼ cup good olive oil

4 cups good bread flour

1 tsp. salt

1 Tbsp. onion chopped (dried or fresh—I use dried)

1 tsp. Italian seasoning

1 tsp. rosemary, dried (plus more
   for sprinkling on top)

extra-virgin olive oil (for rubbing down)

coarse sea salt

1 Tbsp. Parmesan cheese

½ cup grated mozzarella cheese (a blend of
   Romano and mozzarella works as well)

Makes
1 *Large*
or **2** *Small*
Loaves

Istruzioni:

Sprinkle yeast in large bowl. In a large, glass measuring cup, mix warm water with olive oil, then slowly pour over yeast. Mix thoroughly with fork until the yeast is dissolved.

Add sugar to oil/water/yeast mixture and let rest for 5–10 minutes. At this point, you want the chemistry of bubbling to occur.

Add flour, salt, onion, Italian seasoning, and rosemary; mix well. Add in Parmesan and mozzarella cheeses, knead until smooth, and shape into a large ball. Let rest in an oiled bowl until doubled. On a hot day, this should take about 45 minutes, but usually it takes a good hour to rise.

Spray baking sheet, sprinkle with 1 Tbsp. flour, and punch down dough. (At this point you can either divide the dough into halves or make one large round of focaccia.)

Shape loaf or loaves. After placing the dough on the prepared baking sheet, put olive oil in clean hands (not quite a teaspoon, but more than a half teaspoon) and "rub down" the loaves. You can use more olive oil, but you don't want it to drip down around the loaves, just a good rub-down around all 3 sides of the shaped bread dough.

Sprinkle a little more rosemary on top and add the coarse salt sparingly on top, as well. (Because you are using coarse salt, you do not need as much—too much will overpower the focaccia bread). Let dough rise one hour more.

Bake at 400 degrees until brown—about 20 minutes for one loaf; 13–15 minutes for 2 loaves. You will want the tops golden brown. Lightly brush the top of each loaf with extra-virgin olive oil.

✳ ✳ ✳ ✳ ✳ ✳ ✳ ✳ ✳ ✳ ✳ ✳ ✳ ✳ ✳ ✳ ✳ ✳ ✳ ✳

Focaccia is delicious herbed yeast bread eaten with a festive Italian dinner, or for a midnight snack dipped in olive oil … or consumed in inconspicuous bites during Sunday School when the teacher is not looking.

Perfection
Pizza Dough

Perfection Pizza Dough

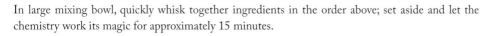

Makes
1 *Large*
or **2** *Medium*
Pizzas

Ingredienti & Istruzioni:

3 tsp. honey (warmed briefly in microwave, about 10 seconds)

1½ cups water

1½ Tbsp. good yeast

In large mixing bowl, quickly whisk together ingredients in the order above; set aside and let the chemistry work its magic for approximately 15 minutes.

After the wet mixture has bubbled, add the following:

3¼–3½ cups unbleached flour

½ tsp. fine sea salt

1 Tbsp. olive oil (plus one or two drops more if too dry)

Mix until the dough can be shaped into a large ball. Let rest and allow 1 hour rising time.

Preheat oven 400 degrees. Spray pizza pan or large baking sheet and lightly dust with flour. Turn dough onto prepared pan and roll to ¼–½ inch thickness.

With fork prongs, randomly indent (but don't entirely pierce) the dough.

Bake 5 minutes.

Remove from oven and cool for 10 minutes. Add pizza sauce (see **Romeo and Juliet Pizza Sauce, page 104**), cheese, and favorite toppings. Return to oven and bake for 20–24 minutes, or until crust is cooked underneath and golden brown.

Pizza is always best cold, the next morning.

Millie's Pumpkin Banana Bread

My Italian mother made many loaves of this bread for
Christmas for *everyone* she knew.

Makes
3
Loaves

Ingredienti:

3½ cups white sugar

5 cups flour

4 tsp. baking soda

¼ tsp. ground cloves

1 cup oil

1½ cups chopped nuts

½ cup brown sugar

1 tsp. salt

2 tsp. cinnamon

1 (29-oz.) can pumpkin

3–4 ripe bananas, mashed

Istruzioni:

Mix all ingredients. Lightly grease three 4.5x8.5 loaf pans. Fill each pan ⅔ full with batter and bake
at 350 degrees for 1½ hours.

The best salt to use in Italian cooking is kosher salt.
Regular table salt has too many additives.

Millie's Pumpkin Banana Bread

Italian Pull-Aparts

※ ※ ※ ※ ※ ※ ※ ※ ※ ※ ※ ※ ※ ※ ※ ※ ※ ※ ※ ※

Makes
4
Servings

Ingredienti:

1 ball of your favorite pizza dough, refrigerated (it
can be store bought – just don't tell your Nona!)

3 Tbsp. butter, melted

½ tsp. garlic salt

¾ tsp. dried rosemary

¾ tsp. dried oregano leaves

Parmesan cheese to taste

Istruzioni:

Roll dough into 14–16 golf-ball sized rounds. Place dough balls in a pie pan or 9x9 casserole dish that is greased with cooking spray. In a separate bowl, mix melted butter and garlic salt. Pour over dough. Sprinkle with rosemary and oregano. Top with Parmesan cheese.

Let rolls rise for 1–2 hours. Bake at 350 degrees for 25–30 minutes. Serve with marinara sauce for dipping.

※ ※ ※ ※ ※ ※ ※ ※ ※ ※ ※ ※ ※ ※ ※ ※ ※ ※ ※ ※

An apple a day may keep the doctor away, but Nona's spaghetti
tastes so much better and keeps me just as happy!

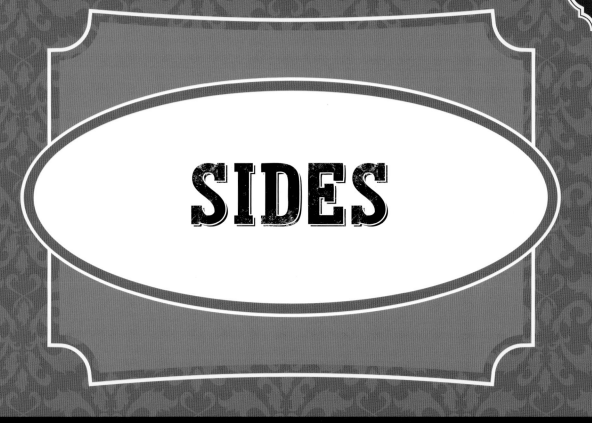

SIDES

Italian Fruit Salad

✳ ✳ ✳ ✳ ✳ ✳ ✳ ✳ ✳ ✳ ✳ ✳ ✳ ✳ ✳ ✳ ✳ ✳ ✳ ✳

Massimo Zanasi, from Bologna, Italy came to stay with us in Ponca City, Oklahoma and made this delicious fruit salad. He later became a chef and is a dear friend we have visited several times in Italy. It is very simple and includes the following fresh fruits:

Makes
8–12
Servings

Ingredienti:

1 pineapple, cubed

1 cantaloupe, cubed

1 quart strawberries, quartered

6 kiwis, cubed

4 bananas, sliced

1 lemon

1 lime

2 Tbsp. sugar (optional)

Istruzioni:

Combine all fruit in a large bowl and squeeze lemon and lime over the top (save bananas until end to avoid browning). Sprinkle with sugar (if desired) and gently blend together. It is beautiful to see and more beautiful to eat.

Buon Appetito!

✳ ✳ ✳ ✳ ✳ ✳ ✳ ✳ ✳ ✳ ✳ ✳ ✳ ✳ ✳ ✳ ✳ ✳ ✳ ✳

No matter how much you knew you'd get in trouble, you still came home from church, stuck half a loaf of bread in the sauce pot, snuck out a fried meatball, and chowed down. You'd make up for it the next week in chores.

Italian
Fruit Salad

Tortellini Salad

Makes **6–8** Servings

Ingredienti:

19 oz. chicken tortellini, cooked according to pkg. directions

6–8 oz. spinach leaves

1 cup grated mozzarella cheese

1 (2.25-oz.) can sliced black olives

3–4 green onions, washed and sliced

6–8 oz. bacon, cooked crisp and crumbled

10 cherry tomatoes, halved

Italian or ranch dressing to taste

Istruzioni:

Rinse and dry spinach leaves, if necessary. Place in a large salad bowl or 9x13 dish. Top with cooked, drained, and cooled tortellini. Garnish with grated cheese, black olives, green onions, bacon, and tomato. Gently toss with dressing of choice.

I told my son when he steps off the plane, returning home from his mission, just follow the smell of spaghetti and meatballs because I will be waiting in the lobby with a plateful.

Orzo and Rice

✳ ✳ ✳ ✳ ✳ ✳ ✳ ✳ ✳ ✳ ✳ ✳ ✳ ✳ ✳ ✳ ✳ ✳ ✳

41

*Makes
enough for
4 Hungry
or **6** Polite
People*

Ingredienti:

1 Tbsp. olive oil

⅓ cup orzo pasta

1 cup rice

2 cups low-sodium chicken broth

¼ cup water

fresh cracked pepper

Parmesan cheese

slivered almonds (optional)

Istruzioni:

In small frying pan, heat olive oil over medium heat. Add orzo pasta and sauté 4–5 minutes, or until golden brown. Stir well.

In large saucepan, bring rice, chicken broth, and water to a boil, then reduce heat to lowest setting. Add sautéed orzo and olive oil, give it a good stir, and then cover with a lid. Let simmer about 20 minutes, or until all the liquid has been absorbed. Then turn off stove and let the covered pan sit for 20 more minutes.

Do not stir again until serving time. Garnish with the remaining ingredients to taste.

✳ ✳ ✳ ✳ ✳ ✳ ✳ ✳ ✳ ✳ ✳ ✳ ✳ ✳ ✳ ✳ ✳ ✳ ✳

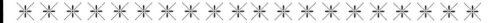

You know you're Italian when: Your grandfather had a fig tree, you eat Sunday dinner at 2 p.m., plastic on the furniture is normal, you've been tapped with a wooden spoon or had a shoe thrown at you, your mom's meatballs are the best, you are on a first-name basis with at least 8 banquet hall owners, and there are more than 28 people in your bridal party.

42

Rocky's Meatballs

✳ ✳

Makes
6–8
Servings

Ingredienti:

1 lb. ground beef

½ lb. ground pork

½ lb. Italian sausage

¾ cup onions, chopped

1 clove garlic, minced

⅓ cup grated Parmesan cheese

1 cup Italian bread crumbs

2 eggs

⅓ cup fresh chopped parsley

1 tsp. sea salt

1 Tbsp. black pepper

¼ cup canola oil

Istruzioni:

Combine beef, pork, sausage, onions, garlic, cheese, bread crumbs, eggs, parsley, sea salt, and pepper. Thoroughly mix. Form into 1½-inch balls. Heat oil in pan. Cook meatballs until done. Serve with red sauce.

✳ ✳

The average Italian is 43 years old.
My great aunt has claimed this age for the last 30 years.

Potatoes Napoli

✳ ✳ ✳ ✳ ✳ ✳ ✳ ✳ ✳ ✳ ✳ ✳ ✳ ✳ ✳ ✳ ✳ ✳ ✳ ✳

Makes **8–10** Servings

43

Ingredienti:

4–4½ pounds russet potatoes, scrubbed and quartered (Yukon gold potatoes are wonderful, too)

½ cup peeled garlic, well chopped (more if you like an extra punch of garlic!)

¾ cup whipping cream or whole milk

3 Tbsp. butter

white pepper to taste

salt to taste

1 generous tsp. rosemary, optional

Parmesan cheese, for serving

Istruzioni:

Place potatoes in a large pot, adding enough water to cover, and bring to a boil. Reduce to simmer until potatoes are tender when pierced with a fork, 15–20 minutes.

In a saucepan over low heat, combine butter, garlic, and cream (or milk). Stir until garlic is tender, 6–8 minutes. Transfer this mixture into a blender or food processor and puree.

Meanwhile, drain your cooked potatoes and place in a large bowl. Hand mash or use an electric mixer. Slowly add the garlic puree. Watch to make sure the potatoes aren't too wet with the puree. If too dry, slowly fold in more milk or butter. Add seasonings.

Garnish with a little Parmesan cheese before serving.

✳ ✳ ✳ ✳ ✳ ✳ ✳ ✳ ✳ ✳ ✳ ✳ ✳ ✳ ✳ ✳ ✳ ✳ ✳ ✳

FHE stands for "Family Home Evening"
and also "Fettuccini Happy Endings."

Baked Sweet
Potato Wedges

Baked Sweet Potato Wedges ✳✳✳✳✳✳✳

Makes **4** Servings

Ingredienti & Instruzioni:

1 pound scrubbed sweet potatoes

Cut off each end of the sweet potatoes and let dry on paper towels. Set aside.

In large mixing bowl whisk well the following:

2 Tbsp. extra virgin olive oil

2 tsp. balsamic vinegar

1½ Tbsp. of Dijon mustard

black pepper to taste (fresh cracked is best)

Cut sweet potatoes in 2-inch wedges; the shape need not be perfect. Thoroughly toss the wedges in the olive oil mixture until the sweet potatoes are well coated.

Preheat oven 350 degrees and prepare a medium-sized baking dish with cooking spray. Pour sweet potatoes into the dish and cover with a lid.

Bake for 45 minutes, or until tender.

✳ ✳ ✳ ✳ ✳ ✳ ✳ ✳ ✳ ✳ ✳ ✳ ✳ ✳ ✳ ✳ ✳ ✳ ✳

Grazie Molto—"Thank you very much."
(Say this to your Nona, and you are guaranteed a second helping.)

46

Chi Chi and Roasted Cumin Salad ✳ ✳ ✳ ✳ ✳ ✳ ✳ ✳ ✳

(Chi Chi beans are garbanzo beans.)

Makes
4
Servings

Ingredienti:

1 generous tsp. ground cumin

2 Tbsp. olive oil

2 Tbsp. lime juice (fresh is best)

salt and pepper to taste

1 (15-oz.) can low-sodium garbanzo beans, drained

1 large stalk celery, washed
and thinly sliced

2 Roma tomatoes, washed and diced

1 small red onion, finely chopped
(use less onion if you desire)

½ cup sliced black olives

1 cup shredded mozzarella, or ½ cup crumbled feta

Istruzioni:

Heat a medium-size frying pan on the stove, then add ground cumin and roast for just a minute or two; stir to keep it from burning.

Place the heated cumin in large mixing bowl. Add the olive oil, lime juice, salt, and pepper. Mix well.

Add all remaining ingredients except cheese.

Toss until well blended. Let the mixture cool for 10–15 minutes. Add cheese and give it one more toss before serving.

✳ ✳ ✳ ✳ ✳ ✳ ✳ ✳ ✳ ✳ ✳ ✳ ✳ ✳ ✳ ✳ ✳ ✳ ✳

For my son's birthday, he didn't want cake—he wanted a meatball the size of a baseball with a birthday candle on it.

Chi Chi and
Roasted Cumin Salad

48

Rosa's Sweet, Sweet Potatoes

Makes
6–8
Servings

Ingredienti:

4 large sweet potatoes, washed and cut into bite-sized pieces

¾–1 cup (1½–2 sticks) unsalted butter, melted

ground cinnamon to taste

freshly grated nutmeg to taste

Istruzioni:

Preheat oven to 400 degrees.

Put sweet potatoes in a large bowl; set aside. Melt butter in saucepan and whisk in the cinnamon and nutmeg.

Drizzle butter mixture over the sweet potatoes and stir to coat evenly. Pour the coated sweet potatoes into a large roasting pan lined with parchment paper. (You can use cooking spray if parchment is unavailable.)

Make sure all pieces are in one layer, spread out well. Roast in oven for 30 minutes, then toss/turn once.

Roast another 30 minutes, or until potatoes are fork tender.

My Italian grandmother used to hide $100 bills, by wrapping them individually
in tin foil and placing them in between ice cube trays. Each semester before I left
for college, she would hand me a few tin foil "money packets" and send me on my way.
My tuition would be "defrosted" by the time I got to campus.

Chad's Famous Asparagus ✳✳✳✳✳✳✳✳✳✳✳✳✳

Makes
4
Servings

Ingredienti:

2 Tbsp. butter

16 asparagus stems, trimmed

2 sprigs fresh rosemary

Parmesan cheese, grated

Istruzioni:

In a sauté pan, melt butter. Add asparagus stems and cook until tender (about 10 minutes on medium heat). Add rosemary about halfway through cooking. Sprinkle with Parmesan cheese (while still in the pan so it melts a bit). Slide onto serving dish with all the extra butter and cheese you can scrape out of the pan!

✳ ✳ ✳ ✳ ✳ ✳ ✳ ✳ ✳ ✳ ✳ ✳ ✳ ✳ ✳ ✳ ✳ ✳ ✳

The best way to eat vegetables is slathered in butter—with cheese!

Caprese Salad

Caprese Salad

✳ ✳ ✳ ✳ ✳ ✳ ✳ ✳ ✳ ✳ ✳ ✳ ✳ ✳ ✳ ✳ ✳ ✳ ✳

Makes
3-4
Servings

Ingredienti:

1 ball (about 1 lb.) of fresh mozzarella cheese, sliced thin

2 ripe red tomatoes, sliced

1 ripe yellow tomato, sliced

12 leaves of basil, washed and torn into small pieces

olive oil

balsamic vinegar

salt and pepper

Istruzioni:

On a large platter, layer alternating pieces of mozzarella, tomatoes, and basil by overlapping the edges of each ingredient. Drizzle with olive oil and balsamic vinegar. Sprinkle with salt and pepper, then serve.

✳ ✳ ✳ ✳ ✳ ✳ ✳ ✳ ✳ ✳ ✳ ✳ ✳ ✳ ✳ ✳ ✳ ✳ ✳

The secret to happiness is a mama's love—and her meatball recipe!

Zucchini Bake

✳ ✳ ✳ ✳ ✳ ✳ ✳ ✳ ✳ ✳ ✳ ✳ ✳ ✳ ✳ ✳ ✳ ✳ ✳

Makes
6
Servings

Ingredienti:

4–5 medium zucchini, washed and dried

1 (14-oz.) can pomodorini (cherry) tomatoes

4 Tbsp. olive oil

1/3 cup fresh parsley, chopped

1 tsp. dried Italian seasonings

2 cloves garlic, finely minced

sea salt and black pepper to taste

dash of red chili flakes (optional)

BREADCRUMB TOPPING

1½ cups small stale country bread cubes

½ cup grated pecorino cheese

zest from half a lemon

½ red chili pepper, chopped (optional)

salt and pepper

2 Tbsp. fresh parsley, chopped

1 Tbsp. olive oil

Istruzioni:

While zucchini casserole is baking, place the bread cubes in a food processor and pulse until they become coarse crumbs. Add chili pepper, lemon, cheese, salt and pepper, and pulse until well blended, but still coarse. Add parsley and olive oil and pulse once more.

Istruzioni:

Preheat oven 375 degrees.

Remove top and tail of zucchini and slice into thin rounds. Place in mixing bowl with the remaining ingredients. Mix well with hands. Pour the zucchini mixture into oven-proof casserole dish large enough to hold everything. Cover and bake for 30 minutes, or until zucchini are fork tender.

Uncover zucchini mixture and sprinkle breadcrumb topping (recipe above) over the top. Return casserole to oven, uncovered, and bake an additional 15 minutes, or until the top is crisp and brown.

✳ ✳ ✳ ✳ ✳ ✳ ✳ ✳ ✳ ✳ ✳ ✳ ✳ ✳ ✳ ✳ ✳ ✳ ✳

The world would be a more peaceful place if friends
and neighbors consumed more pasta together.

PASTA

Creamy Ragu Bolognese

✳ ✳ ✳ ✳ ✳ ✳ ✳ ✳ ✳ ✳ ✳ ✳ ✳ ✳ ✳ ✳ ✳ ✳ ✳

Makes **6–8** *Servings*

Ingredienti:

¼ cup olive oil

1 large sweet onion, finely chopped

1 large carrot, finely chopped

1 lb. ground or chopped beef

½ lb. ground pork

4 slices bacon, cooked and chopped

1 (28-oz.) can diced tomatoes

1 (8-oz.) container heavy cream, divided

2 cups beef broth

1 Tbsp. garlic powder

1 lb. pasta

Istruzioni:

Cook onion and carrot in olive oil until soft. Set aside.

In a large pan, cook beef and pork. Break into small lumps as it cooks. Drain. Return meats, onion, and carrot to large pan. Add cooked bacon. Stir in ½ container of cream. Simmer until absorbed. Stir in tomatoes. Simmer 10 minutes. Add beef broth. Sprinkle in garlic powder. Add salt and pepper to taste. Simmer sauce at least 1½ hours; it should be fairly thick.

Just before serving, add remaining cream. Cook and drain pasta. Toss with sauce. Serve with parmigiano-reggiano cheese.

✳ ✳ ✳ ✳ ✳ ✳ ✳ ✳ ✳ ✳ ✳ ✳ ✳ ✳ ✳ ✳ ✳ ✳ ✳

You will never hear an Italian say, "This dish has too many onions."
No such thing.

Spaghetti Alla Carbonara

✳ ✳ ✳ ✳ ✳ ✳ ✳ ✳ ✳ ✳ ✳ ✳ ✳ ✳ ✳ ✳ ✳ ✳

Makes **6–8** *Servings*

Ingredienti:

1 lb. bacon, sliced in small pieces

3–4 green onions, chopped

2–3 eggs, beaten with a fork in separate bowl

1 cup fresh-grated Parmesan cheese, divided

1–1½ cups cream

¼–½ tsp. ground black pepper

1 lb. spaghetti (or desired pasta)

2 Tbsp. butter

pinch of kosher salt

Istruzioni:

Start water for pasta boiling with a pinch of salt in a large pot. In separate pan, fry bacon until semi-cooked and then drain grease. Add chopped green onions to bacon and continue cooking until bacon and green onions are golden brown. Set aside. In the mixing bowl with beaten eggs, add half the Parmesan cheese, all of the cream, and pepper. Stir together and set aside.

Add pasta to boiling water. Cook and drain. Return hot pasta to pot, adding butter, and place back on burner (turned off or to very low). Add egg mixture and remaining Parmesan cheese to hot pasta and gently stir. At first sign of eggs cooking, add green onions and bacon, and it is done. Serve in warm bowls—it is delicious and filling! *Buon appetito!*

✳ ✳ ✳ ✳ ✳ ✳ ✳ ✳ ✳ ✳ ✳ ✳ ✳ ✳ ✳ ✳ ✳ ✳

This recipe comes from Marisa Zanasi. It was sold on the street and cooked on coal fires in earlier times. It is a very rich and flavorful pasta dish. We loved dining with the Zanasi's—their brightness and warmth filled our hearts and their delicious pastas filled our tummies.

Christopher's Potato Gnocchi

✳ ✳ ✳ ✳ ✳ ✳ ✳ ✳ ✳ ✳ ✳ ✳ ✳ ✳ ✳ ✳ ✳ ✳ ✳ ✳

Drenched in sauce or fried in butter, gnocchi is true comfort food. These little dumplings are a fun way to introduce young chefs to the world of pasta making. Make them once to get the hang of it, and after that you will be a pro.

Makes
6–8
Servings

Ingredienti:

2 lbs. russet potatoes, scrubbed
  and pierced to let heat escape

2 egg yokes, beaten

fine sea salt to taste

1¼–1½ cups flour (add enough
  for a dough consistency)

Istruzioni:

Bake potatoes until done in 375 degree oven (about 50 minutes). When cooled enough to touch, slice in half horizontally.

With large spoon, remove potatoes from their skins and place in a medium-sized mixing bowl. Mix well by hand—you do not want lumps. (I do not recommend using an electric mixer.) While the potatoes are still warm, add the egg and salt. Slowly add in the flour. Do not over-work the mixture. You want a moist ball of dough.

Lightly dust your prep board or countertop with flour. I keep a small bowl of "finger flour" nearby for the following process:

Divide dough into about six pieces. With your fingertips, *gently* roll each piece into "snakes" about ¾-inch wide. Cut each snake into one-inch pieces. For cooking purposes, try to keep each cut piece the same size.

With a fork, press each one-inch gnocchi piece into the tines—enough to indent, but do not go completely through the dough. Place on a floured surface, board, or baking sheet. The indention makes a little curvature that is meant to catch the sauce in the serving process.

Bring a large pot of water to boil then reduce the heat to medium-high. Gently drop in a few gnocchi at a time and cook for about 4–5 minutes. When they are done they rise to the surface. Remove the cooked gnocchi with a large, slotted spoon and drain. Cover them to keep warm. Serve with your favorite sauce and cheese.

Gnocchi can also be fried in butter until golden brown. If this method is used, toss with added butter and Parmesan cheese.

This recipe makes a huge batch—so invite Nona over! It also freezes well.

✳ ✳ ✳ ✳ ✳ ✳ ✳ ✳ ✳ ✳ ✳ ✳ ✳ ✳ ✳ ✳ ✳ ✳ ✳ ✳

What do you call an Italian with his hands in his pocket?
ANSWER: A mute.

Christopher's
Potato Gnocchi

Linguine Carbonara

✳ ✳ ✳ ✳ ✳ ✳ ✳ ✳ ✳ ✳ ✳ ✳ ✳ ✳ ✳ ✳ ✳ ✳ ✳

Makes **4** *Servings*

Ingredienti:

8 oz. linguine pasta, cooked

1 egg, lightly beaten

1¼ cups evaporated milk

⅓ green pepper, sliced

⅛ tsp. red pepper flakes

⅛ tsp. ground black pepper

½ tsp. garlic powder

½ cup grated Parmesan cheese

¾ cup frozen peas, thawed

3 strips bacon, cooked and crumbled

6 oz. (or three links) chicken Italian sausage, cooked

½ cup of artichoke hearts, sliced

2 Tbsp. cilantro, chopped

Istruzioni:

In a saucepan, cook the following on medium heat: egg, milk, green pepper, red pepper flakes, black pepper, and garlic powder. When mixture is heated thoroughly, add cheese, peas, bacon, sausage, artichoke hearts, and cilantro. Mix well on low to medium heat until sauce lightly bubbles.

Serve over cooked pasta.

✳ ✳ ✳ ✳ ✳ ✳ ✳ ✳ ✳ ✳ ✳ ✳ ✳ ✳ ✳ ✳ ✳ ✳ ✳

FAMOUS ITALIANS:
Sophia Loren—Actress
Christopher Columbus—Explorer
Michelangelo—Sculptor and painter
Giorgio Armani—Fashion Designer

Linguine Carbonara

Spinach and Sundried Tomato Lasagna ✳ ✳ ✳ ✳ ✳ ✳ ✳ ✳

Makes
6–8
Servings

Ingredienti:

3 cups ricotta cheese

2 eggs

½ cup grated Parmesan cheese (divided)

½ tsp. oregano

1 Tbsp. dried onion

1 tsp. crumbled sweet basil leaves

1 cup chopped spinach (fresh or frozen; make sure frozen is well drained)

1 lb. shredded mozzarella, divided

¼ cup grated Romano cheese

1 cup sundried tomatoes drained (use ones that are julienne cut in olive oil with herbs)

1 lb. dry lasagna or 9 oz. no-cook lasagna sheets (If using dried lasagna, follow the cooking instructions on box.)

approx. 6 cups of your favorite red sauce

meat mixture (see next column):

MEAT MIXTURE:

1 pound ground sirloin, cooked and drained

1 (7-oz.) can of mushrooms, drained (stems and pieces) or ½ cup fresh chopped mushrooms

garlic to taste

pepper to taste

1 (2.25-oz.) can of sliced black olives, drained

✳ ✳ ✳ ✳ ✳ ✳ ✳ ✳ ✳ ✳ ✳ ✳ ✳ ✳ ✳ ✳ ✳ ✳

One of the most valuable phrases in Italy:
"Complimenti alla cuoca" (compliments to the cook).

Istruzioni:

Spray deep-dish lasagna pan with cooking spray. Preheat oven 350 degrees.

In mixing bowl blend well the following ingredients: Ricotta cheese, eggs, ¼ cup Parmesan cheese, oregano, dried onion, and sweet basil. Add salt and pepper to taste. Set mixture aside.

In the bottom of prepared baking dish spread thin layer of red sauce, then layer in the following order:

LASAGNA PASTA OR SHEETS

I CUP OF RICOTTA MIXTURE (SPREAD EVENLY ACROSS PAN)

I CUP MOZZARELLA (SPREAD EVENLY ACROSS PAN)

ALL OF THE MEAT MIXTURE

ANOTHER LAYER OF LASAGNA

THIN LAYER OF RED SAUCE

I CUP RICOTTA MIXTURE

LAYER OF SPINACH

I CUP MOZZARELLA

LAYER OF LASAGNA

THIN LAYER OF RED SAUCE

REMAINING RICOTTA MIXTURE

SUNDRIED TOMATOES (SPREAD EVENLY)

LAST LAYER OF LASAGNA

REMAINING RED SAUCE

REMAINING MOZZARELLA

¼ CUP PARMESAN CHEESE

ROMANO CHEESE

Bake covered for 1 hour and 15 minutes. Uncover and bake for 10 more minutes.

SHANNON'S NOTE: Depending on the pan size, the thickness of the lasagna layers may vary. Using a deeper pan, you may need to use another ½ to a full box of lasagna pasta.

Macaroni
and Cheese

Macaroni and Cheese

Makes
4
Servings

Ingredienti:

2 cups elbow macaroni

1 (12-oz.) can evaporated milk

salt and pepper to taste

1 block (1½ lbs.) sharp cheddar cheese, grated, divided

paprika to taste

¼ cup bread crumbs

Istruzioni:

Preheat oven to 325 degrees.

Cook macaroni in salted water according to directions on the box, then drain. Place hot macaroni in a buttered baking dish. Pour evaporated milk over pasta; mix in salt and pepper. Add ⅔ of cheese to the macaroni mixture. Mix well. Sprinkle with remaining cheese and top with paprika for color. Top with bread crumbs. Bake for 1 hour. Cool and serve.

One pot + one baking dish = simple comfort food.

Stuffed Manicotti

✳ ✳ ✳ ✳ ✳ ✳ ✳ ✳ ✳ ✳ ✳ ✳ ✳ ✳ ✳ ✳ ✳ ✳

Makes
4
Servings

Ingredienti:

2 cups cooked chopped spinach
  (fresh or frozen), well drained

1½–2 cups ricotta cheese

1 egg

½ tsp. garlic

1 tsp. salt

pepper to taste

4–5 cups of your favorite
  marinara sauce

1 lb. ground beef (you could also
  add some Italian sausage)

dehydrated onions to taste

Italian seasoning to taste

Parmesan cheese to taste

8 manicotti pasta, cooked al dente

Istruzioni:

In a bowl, mix well the following: spinach, ricotta, egg, garlic, salt, and pepper. Set aside. In a pan, cook beef (and sausage, if used), onion, and spices thoroughly. Drain and let cool. Blend ricotta and meat mixture together. Stuff manicotti tubes with mixture and place in pan or baking dish. Cover with marinara sauce and Parmesan cheese. Bake for 20–25 minutes at 350 degrees.

✳ ✳ ✳ ✳ ✳ ✳ ✳ ✳ ✳ ✳ ✳ ✳ ✳ ✳ ✳ ✳ ✳ ✳

It wasn't until college, living with roommates, that I learned
that not all people eat pasta four times a week.

Mom's Simple Lasagna

Makes
6
Servings

Ingredienti:

1 box lasagna pasta

2 small eggs

2 cups cooked chopped spinach (fresh or frozen), well drained

2 cups ricotta cheese

1 cup Parmesan cheese, divided

2 cups grated mozzarella cheese, divided

6 cups red sauce (use your favorite), divided

Istruzioni:

Preheat oven to 350 degrees. Cook pasta according to instructions on box, and then drain.

In separate bowl, beat two eggs and add spinach, ricotta cheese, half the Parmesan cheese, and half the mozzarella cheese. In buttered baking dish, start with one layer of sauce, one layer of pasta, one layer of ricotta cheese mixture, and one layer of mozzarella cheese. Repeat until pan is filled. Top with remaining mozzarella and Parmesan cheeses. Bake for 2 hours. Cool and serve.

✳ ✳ ✳ ✳ ✳ ✳ ✳ ✳ ✳ ✳ ✳ ✳ ✳ ✳ ✳ ✳ ✳ ✳ ✳ ✳

An Italian table is set with any dishes that are in the cupboard ...
it doesn't matter if they don't match. They're clean, that's all that matters.

Vegetarian Stuffed Manicotti

✳ ✳ ✳ ✳ ✳ ✳ ✳ ✳ ✳ ✳ ✳ ✳ ✳ ✳ ✳ ✳ ✳ ✳ ✳ ✳

Makes
6–8
Servings

Ingredienti:

1 (8-oz.) box (or half a 1-lb. bag)
frozen chopped spinach

1 (8-oz.) box manicotti tubes

2 Tbsp. olive oil

1 (30-oz.) container ricotta cheese

2 cups imported grated Romano (can
be purchased at the deli counter)

4 cups grated mozzarella, divided

1 egg

2 tsp. garlic powder

2 tsp. onion powder

1 tsp. basil

1 tsp. Italian seasoning

1 tsp. pepper

3–4 cups of your favorite marinara sauce

Istruzioni:

Thaw spinach in strainer. Wrap spinach in paper towels to remove all excess water. Preheat oven to 350 degrees. Cook manicotti pasta (follow directions on box; make sure to add a little olive oil to cooking water); set aside and cool. In large bowl, mix ricotta, spinach, Romano, 2 cups of the grated mozzarella, egg, and all seasonings. Stuff manicotti with ricotta mixture. Coat 9x13 glass baking dish with cooking spray. Cover the bottom of the baking dish with a little of the marinara. Add stuffed manicotti on top of sauce, then pour remaining sauce over the stuffed manicotti tubes. Top with remaining mozzarella cheese. Cover with foil and cook for 30 minutes, or until hot and cheese is melted.

This recipe can be prepared and refrigerated (uncooked) overnight for an easy dinner the next day.

✳ ✳ ✳ ✳ ✳ ✳ ✳ ✳ ✳ ✳ ✳ ✳ ✳ ✳ ✳ ✳ ✳ ✳ ✳ ✳

My Italian family eats a half a pound of bread a day—a pound on
the Sabbath because that is the day Grandpa comes over for dinner!

Tommy's Spaghetti with Meatballs & Sausages ✳ ✳ ✳ ✳

Makes
6–8
Servings

67

Ingredienti:

1 lb. lean ground beef

1 egg

1 cup Italian bread crumbs

¼ cup Parmesan cheese

2 Tbsp. fresh chopped parsley

½ tsp. black pepper

½ tsp. kosher salt

1 lb. Italian sausages

olive oil

5–6 cups marinara sauce

Istruzioni:

Combine all of the ingredients except the Italian sausage, olive oil, and red sauce. (It's easiest, and more Italian, to mix using your hands). Add a few tablespoons of water to the mixture, until it feels wet. (If you don't add enough water, your meatballs will get rock hard.) Form into balls.

Cover the bottom of a large frying pan with olive oil. Turn the stove to medium heat. Add the sausages to the oil and turn every minute or two until the sausage browns. (They don't need to be cooked thoroughly at this point.) Remove the sausages from the pan and put on a plate. Brown the meatballs, a few at a time, in the oil. (You just want them to brown, not cook all the way.) Return Italian sausage to the frying pan with the meatballs; add your favorite red sauce and simmer until meat is cooked thoroughly. Serve over spaghetti or bread.

This recipe is an Italian family favorite. It is great for a Sunday family dinner at home or when the extended family gets together at the shore or lake.

Why don't Italians have freckles?
They all slide off.

Tomato and Olive Pasta

✳ ✳ ✳ ✳ ✳ ✳ ✳ ✳ ✳ ✳ ✳ ✳ ✳ ✳ ✳ ✳ ✳ ✳ ✳

Makes
4–6
Servings

Ingredienti:

¼ cup extra virgin olive oil

1 large sweet onion, thickly sliced

1 (28-oz.) can diced tomatoes

¼ cup water

1 Tbsp. garlic powder

1 tsp. oregano flakes

10 oz. angel hair pasta,
  cooked and drained

1 lb. large black sicilian olives, pitted and chopped

black pepper

parmigianno-reggiano cheese

Istruzioni:

Cook onion in oil until soft, not brown. Add chopped tomatoes and water. Add garlic powder and oregano. Cook sauce over medium heat until it thickens (about 30 minutes). Stir frequently. Pour sauce over cooked pasta, adding olives last. Toss. Sprinkle with freshly ground black pepper. Serve with parmigianno-reggiano cheese.

✳ ✳ ✳ ✳ ✳ ✳ ✳ ✳ ✳ ✳ ✳ ✳ ✳ ✳ ✳ ✳ ✳ ✳ ✳

"Art is never finished, only abandoned."
—Leonardo da Vinci

Tomato and
Olive Pasta

Pasta Puttanesca

✳ ✳ ✳ ✳ ✳ ✳ ✳ ✳ ✳ ✳ ✳ ✳ ✳ ✳ ✳ ✳ ✳ ✳ ✳

Ingredienti:

¼ cup olive oil

1 medium onion, chopped finely

1 Tbsp. garlic, chopped

½ tsp. salt

¼ tsp. white pepper

2 grinds of black pepper

dash of red pepper flakes

1 Tbsp. Italian Seasoning

1 tsp. parsley flakes

1 Tbsp. anchovy paste

¼ cup vegetable broth or water

1 (6-oz.) can tomato paste

1 (28-oz.) can chopped tomatoes

1 cup kalamata olives, coarsely chopped

¼ cup capers

1 lb. spaghetti pasta, cooked al dente (reserve cooking water)

Parmesan cheese, to garnish

Makes 6–8 Servings

Istruzioni:

Heat oil in a large sauté pan over medium-low heat. Add onion and garlic. Season with salt, white pepper, black pepper, red pepper flakes, Italian seasoning, and parsley. Cook until onions and garlic are tender, around 10 minutes, stirring frequently. Remove pan from heat. Stir in anchovy paste, tomato paste, and broth or water. Mixture will be thick. Next, add in canned tomatoes and mix well. Turn the heat to low and stir in olives and capers. Return pan to very low heat and cover with a lid. Let it simmer on low for 30–45 minutes.

In a large bowl, combine cooked pasta and two large spoonfuls of sauce. Toss well to coat. If pasta is starting to stick together, add some of the salted pasta water from the pot the pasta was cooked in.

Assemble pasta on a large plate or bowl. Top with Puttanesca sauce and Parmesan cheese.

The best thing about this pasta is that the longer it sits, the more flavorful it becomes.

✳ ✳ ✳ ✳ ✳ ✳ ✳ ✳ ✳ ✳ ✳ ✳ ✳ ✳ ✳ ✳ ✳ ✳ ✳

When I pack my lunch, I have to put it in a large paper grocery bag so that the meatballs, pasta, mozzarella slices, stuffed mushrooms and homemade chocolate truffles all fit!

Pasta e Fagioli

Makes **8** *Servings*

Ingredienti:

olive oil

½ lb. lean ground Italian sausage (mild)

1 lb. lean ground beef

¾ tsp. pepper

¾ tsp. dried sweet basil, crushed

¾ tsp. oregano

½ tsp. sugar

1 (1-oz.) envelope dried onion soup mix

6½ cups water

1 (15-oz.) can tomato sauce

1 (15-oz.) can kidney beans, drained

1 (15-oz.) can red beans, mostly drained (mix in a little of the "gravy")

1 cup chopped celery (about 3 stalks)

1½ cups dried small pasta shells or small elbow pasta

Istruzioni:

In large, deep frying pan (have lid handy) drizzle olive oil, give it a whirl around the pan. Cook and brown meats thoroughly, draining off most of the fat (leaving a little is okay).

Add into pan: seasonings, sugar, dry soup mix, water, and tomato sauce, stir together mixing well. Cover with lid and simmer for 15 minutes.

Add beans, celery and pasta, blending them well in the pan. Turn heat up to just boiling, stir again making sure nothing is sticking to the bottom of pan and reduce heat to low. Cover with lid and simmer for 20 minutes, or until pasta is completely cooked.

Serve with a crusty bread. Garnish with shredded cheese.

Pappardelle is long, broad, flat ribbons of pasta.
"Pappare" in Italian means to gobble up.

72

"Second Helping Please" Pasta and Vegetables ✳ ✳ ✳

Makes **8** *Servings*

Ingredienti:

extra-virgin olive oil

2 cloves garlic, crushed

½ cup chopped red onion

½ cup chopped celery

½ cup chopped carrot

2 medium tomatoes, chopped

1 (4-oz.) can sliced mushrooms, drained

1 small red bell pepper, julienne sliced

2½ cups (20 oz.) chicken stock, either homemade or low-sodium organic

freshly ground pepper and salt to taste

1 (1-lb.) box penne pasta, cooked according to pkg. directions

1 cup frozen peas (defrost in warm water or let sit at room temperature)

olive oil, for drizzling

shaved Parmesan cheese, for garnish

Istruzioni:

Heat a large pot with a lid over medium heat and drizzle oil to coat the pan. When the oil just begins to bubble, add the garlic and onion and cook for about 5 minutes. (You may need to turn the heat down a bit.) Add the celery and carrot; cook for another 3 minutes. Add the tomatoes, mushrooms, and bell pepper and cook for another 2 minutes. Add chicken stock and seasoning.

Simmer together about 10 minutes. Add cooked, drained penne pasta to the pot and toss. Add the peas and heat through. Then plate onto a serving platter, drizzle with olive oil and garnish with shaved Parmesan cheese, and serve!

VARIATION: Substitute your favorite vegetables in place of those listed. You can also add 2 cups of cooked chicken, cubed.

Italian cooking and preferences are very much regional.
In northern Italy, butter is more commonly used over olive oil;
rice and corn are also more used than pasta.

Pesto Pasta

✳ ✳ ✳ ✳ ✳ ✳ ✳ ✳ ✳ ✳ ✳ ✳ ✳ ✳ ✳ ✳ ✳ ✳ ✳ ✳

Makes
3–4
Servings

Ingredienti:

2¼ cup flour

3 eggs

1 Tbsp. extra virgin olive oil

¼ cup pesto (use whatever is your favorite)

Istruzioni:

Place flour in a mixing bowl. Make a well in the middle of the flour. Add eggs, olive oil, and pesto in the well. Slowly mix eggs, oil, and pesto into flour with a spoon. Knead dough. Roll dough into ball and wrap with plastic wrap. Refrigerate for about an hour, until dough becomes firm.

Roll dough out, as thin as possible, on a floured surface. Cut the dough into long, narrow strips with a knife (or you can use a pasta maker). Let pasta dry for one hour.

Cook and serve with your favorite sauce.

✳ ✳ ✳ ✳ ✳ ✳ ✳ ✳ ✳ ✳ ✳ ✳ ✳ ✳ ✳ ✳ ✳ ✳ ✳ ✳

Italian Rule of Thumb: Never trust a thin cook.

Mama's Spaghetti
and Meatballs

Mama's Spaghetti and Meatballs ✳✳✳✳✳✳✳✳✳

Makes
6
Servings

Ingredienti:

MEATBALLS:

¾ lb. ground beef

½ lb. sausage

1 cup fine dry bread crumbs

½ cup grated Parmesan cheese

1 Tbsp. dry parsley

2 small garlic cloves, finely chopped

½ cup milk

2 eggs, beaten

salt and pepper to taste

4 Tbsp. olive oil

Ingredienti:

SAUCE:

2 Tbsp. flour

5 cups cooked tomatoes

3 Tbsp. minced parsley

6 Tbsp. minced green pepper

2 tsp. salt

¼ tsp. pepper

3 Tbsp. sugar

2 small bay leaves, crumbled

1 Tbsp. Worcestershire sauce

Istruzioni for Meatballs:

Mix all ingredients except olive oil, and form into balls. Flatten slightly at the top. Pan fry in olive oil until brown.

Istruzioni for Sauce:

In the same frying pan used for frying the meatballs, whisk flour in remaining olive oil. Add the tomatoes, parsley, green pepper, salt, pepper, sugar, bay leaves, and Worcestershire sauce. Simmer one hour. Serve over cooked spaghetti pasta. Sprinkle with Parmesan cheese.

✳✳✳✳✳✳✳✳✳✳✳✳✳✳✳✳✳✳✳✳

Growing up, Nona called all pasta "spaghetti."

Simple Creamy Fettuccini

Simple Creamy Fettuccini

✳ ✳

Makes
4–6
Servings

Ingredienti:

½ cup of butter

1 cup whipping cream (but don't whip it
 —use straight from the carton)

1 cup sour cream

salt and pepper

12 oz. fettuccini pasta

3 Roma tomatoes, chopped

Parmesan cheese

Istruzioni:

Melt butter in a saucepan. Add whipping cream and sour cream; stir on medium heat until thoroughly blended and warm. Add salt and pepper. Cook fettuccini according to package directions; drain. Place pasta in serving bowl. Pour sauce on top. Garnish with tomatoes and cheese.

✳ ✳

"Esse nufesso qui dice male di macaroni."
(Translation: He who speaks badly of macaroni is a fool.)

Parmesan Artichoke Pasta

✳ ✳ ✳ ✳ ✳ ✳ ✳ ✳ ✳ ✳ ✳ ✳ ✳ ✳ ✳ ✳ ✳ ✳ ✳ ✳

Makes
4–6
Servings

Ingredienti:

2½ cups of milk

2 Tbsp. butter

¼ cup of all-purpose flour

½ tsp. garlic powder

⅓ cup of Parmesan cheese

1 (6.5-oz.) jar artichoke hearts, drained and coarsely chopped

4–6 leaves fresh basil, chopped

salt and pepper to taste

cooked pasta

Istruzioni:

In a large frying pan, warm the milk on low-medium heat. Melt butter in a small saucepan. Add flour to the butter, making a roux. Stir for about one minute, but do not let the roux brown or overcook. Remove roux from heat and combine with milk in frying pan. Stir continuously for about 1 minute to get rid of any lumps. Bring to a boil, stirring often. When sauce is thick, turn heat down to low. Add garlic powder, Parmesan cheese, artichoke hearts, and fresh basil. Simmer for 3–4 minutes. Sprinkle with salt and pepper to taste.

Add sauce to cooked pasta.

✳ ✳ ✳ ✳ ✳ ✳ ✳ ✳ ✳ ✳ ✳ ✳ ✳ ✳ ✳ ✳ ✳ ✳ ✳ ✳

An Italian garden isn't complete without
basil and tomatoes—AND cute gardening shoes!

Parmesan Artichoke Pasta

Riguetel Sauce & Whole-Wheat Pasta ✳ ✳ ✳ ✳ ✳

Makes
8–10
Servings

From my friend, Karen Jannuzzi: Grandma Rosalba Jannuzzi made this meal for all special occasions and I still make it for my husband's birthday every year. The whole-wheat pasta is the secret to this recipe. Regular pasta just doesn't have the same texture and taste. I have found that whole-wheat elbow macaroni is now available and is a passable substitute for the homemade pasta, but we still like grandma's recipe best.

Ingredienti:

¼ cup onion, diced

2 lbs. pork ribs, cut into chunks

2 lbs. beef ribs, cut into chunks

2 lbs. lamb, cut into chunks

2 quarts tomatoes

2 (12-oz.) cans tomato paste

salt, sugar, and basil to taste

1½ lb. whole-wheat elbow macaroni, cooked
(you could also use orecchiette,
radiatore, penne, or rigatoni)

Istruzioni:

Brown onion and meats in olive oil in a large pot. Add tomatoes, tomato paste, and spices. Simmer on low heat all day. Serve over whole-wheat pasta.

✳ ✳ ✳ ✳ ✳ ✳ ✳ ✳ ✳ ✳ ✳ ✳ ✳ ✳ ✳ ✳ ✳ ✳ ✳

If you don't like Mama's pasta—you need your noodle examined.

MAIN DISHES

Italian Roast Chicken

✳ ✳ ✳ ✳ ✳ ✳ ✳ ✳ ✳ ✳ ✳ ✳ ✳ ✳ ✳ ✳ ✳ ✳

Makes **4–6** *Servings*

Ingredienti:

¼ cup grape seed oil

4–5 lbs. whole chicken

sea salt to taste

freshly ground black pepper to taste

2 small lemons, cut in half

1 medium onion, cut in quarters

4 (or more) cloves of garlic

several sprigs of fresh flat-leaf parsley

5 small sprigs fresh rosemary

Istruzioni:

Preheat oven to 375 degrees. Rub roasting pan with grape seed oil on all sides. Discard chicken parts from cavity of chicken, and then wash and pat dry. Sprinkle chicken cavity with salt and pepper and fresh-squeezed lemon juice, inside and out. Add onions, garlic, parsley, and rosemary to inside of the chicken.

Tie legs together with cooking twine. Rub grape seed oil over the body of the chicken.

Roast for one hour and baste with juices. Baste again 15 minutes later, and once more before serving. Total roasting time should be 1½ hours.

✳ ✳ ✳ ✳ ✳ ✳ ✳ ✳ ✳ ✳ ✳ ✳ ✳ ✳ ✳ ✳ ✳ ✳

Prom dress that Aunt Rosa made you: $21.00 for material.
Prom hair-do from Cousin Angela: Free.
Turning around at prom to see your entire family (including grandparents
and senile Great-Uncle Antonio) standing in the back of the gym: PRICELESS!

"Kitchen" Cacciatore

Makes
6
Servings

Ingredienti:

2½–3 lbs. of chicken fryer, cut up; or all breast pieces is fine (for a healthier meal, I remove skins, but many prefer skins on)

¼ cup good olive oil

½ cup flour

2 onions, sliced in rings

1 chopped green pepper

2 cloves garlic, crushed or finely chopped

1 (16-oz.) can sliced stewed tomatoes, drained

1 (8-oz.) can tomato sauce

1 (3-oz.) can sliced mushrooms, drained (or 4 large fresh mushrooms, well scrubbed and sliced)

1 tsp. salt

½ tsp. oregano

Istruzioni:

Wash chicken and pat dry. Heat olive oil in large skillet. Coat chicken with flour. Cook chicken in oil over medium heat for 15–20 minutes or until light brown, turning with tongs.

Remove cooked chicken from skillet and set aside. Add onion, green pepper, and garlic to the skillet. Stir and cook until they are tender. Add remaining ingredients. This makes the sauce.

After sauce is well blended, add chicken back into skillet. Cover with a tight lid. Simmer for 35–45 minutes, or until the thickest pieces of the chicken are fork tender.

Serve with cooked orzo, rice, or linguine.

As a young girl, I thought this recipe was called
"kitchen cacciatore" instead of "chicken cacciatore."
My grandmother's Italian accent was to blame.

Nanny's Simple Roast

✳ ✳ ✳ ✳ ✳ ✳ ✳ ✳ ✳ ✳ ✳ ✳ ✳ ✳ ✳ ✳ ✳ ✳ ✳

Makes
6–8
Servings

Ingredienti:

3–4 lbs. beef roast

lemon juice to taste

garlic powder to taste

pepper to taste

paprika to taste

Istruzioni:

Preheat oven to 350 degrees. Place roast on cooking rack in a large pan. Sprinkle lemon juice, garlic powder, pepper, and paprika all over the roast. Cover with foil. Bake 30 minutes for each pound of roast. This is delicious with my **Baked Sweet Potato Wedges (see page 45)** or **Orzo and Rice (see page 41)**.

✳ ✳ ✳ ✳ ✳ ✳ ✳ ✳ ✳ ✳ ✳ ✳ ✳ ✳ ✳ ✳ ✳ ✳ ✳

This recipe holds many fond memories for our family!

Nanny's Simple Roast

Sicilian Meatloaf

✳ ✳ ✳ ✳ ✳ ✳ ✳ ✳ ✳ ✳ ✳ ✳ ✳ ✳ ✳ ✳ ✳ ✳ ✳

Makes
6–8
Servings

Ingredienti:

1 lb. ground turkey (or 1 lb. ground sirloin)

1 lb. hot and spicy Italian sausage

2 celery stalks, sliced

1 cup Italian bread crumbs

1 egg

5 oz. hot and spicy V-8 Juice

¼ cup honey

1 small brown onion, chopped fine

1 small zucchini, grated

1 Tbsp. garlic salt

2 Tbsp. minced garlic

2 Tbsp. ground black pepper

1 Tbsp. celery salt

Istruzioni:

Preheat oven to 350 degrees. Mix all the ingredients thoroughly in large bowl. Shape into loaf and put in a pan coated with cooking spray. Cover with foil. Cooking time is approximately 1 hour and 15 minutes. Remove from oven, let stand for 10 minutes, and then slice.

✳ ✳ ✳ ✳ ✳ ✳ ✳ ✳ ✳ ✳ ✳ ✳ ✳ ✳ ✳ ✳ ✳ ✳ ✳

Meatballs must always be made by hand.

Juicy Italian Baked Chicken ✳ ✳ ✳ ✳ ✳ ✳ ✳ ✳

Makes
4–6
Servings

Ingredienti:

4–6 small red potatoes, whole

1 large onion, sliced

4 Roma tomatoes, chopped, or
  1 (14-oz.) can chopped tomatoes

2–3 cloves of pressed garlic

salt and pepper to taste

½ cup extra virgin olive oil

1 Tbsp. of oregano

1 cup chopped Italian parsley

1 whole chicken, cut up (or 4-6 large chicken breasts)

2 (14-oz.) cans of peas, or 1 (28-oz.) bag
  of frozen peas, thawed

Istruzioni:

Preheat oven to 350 degrees. Mix all ingredients (except chicken and peas) in a bowl. Place chicken in baking dish. Pour mixture over chicken. Cover with foil and bake 30 minutes, remove foil and continue to bake an hour longer. During the last 10 minutes of baking, add peas. Before taking out of oven, make sure potatoes are done by piercing with a fork.

✳ ✳ ✳ ✳ ✳ ✳ ✳ ✳ ✳ ✳ ✳ ✳ ✳ ✳ ✳ ✳ ✳ ✳ ✳

When you swap recipes with an Italian—NEVER ask them about
the "number of servings" a dish makes, if it is not already listed
on the instructions. Most Italians live by the rule to make a
ton of food so people can eat until they are stuffed.

Tuscan Tomato Pie

Tuscan Tomato Pie

✳ ✳ ✳ ✳ ✳ ✳ ✳ ✳ ✳ ✳ ✳ ✳ ✳ ✳ ✳ ✳ ✳ ✳ ✳

Makes
6
Servings

Ingredienti:

1 baked piecrust (still warm from the oven)

½ lb. sliced mozzarella

3 tomatoes, thinly sliced

pinch of minced garlic

½ cup dry bread crumbs (seasoned or plain;
   I prefer seasoned), divided

fresh chopped basil

Parmesan cheese

Istruzioni:

While piecrust is still warm, layer slices of mozzarella cheese in the bottom of the pie crust. Then top with tomatoes, garlic (to taste), a thin layer of dried bread crumbs (about a ¼ cup—just a thin layer), basil (to taste), Parmesan, and sliced mozzarella.

Repeat the entire process, beginning with the thinly sliced tomatoes. Make sure your final topping is the Parmesan and mozzarella cheese.

Cover with foil. Bake for 20–25 minutes at 375 degrees.

✳ ✳ ✳ ✳ ✳ ✳ ✳ ✳ ✳ ✳ ✳ ✳ ✳ ✳ ✳ ✳ ✳ ✳ ✳

I'm convinced that the Italian's best idea was the invention of pizza pie.
I'm also convinced that my mother's best idea was to feed it to us weekly.

Uncle Dale's Eggplant Parmesan

Makes
6-8
Servings

Ingredienti:

2 eggplants, peeled and thinly sliced

2 eggs, beaten

4 cups flour

6 cups pasta sauce— marinara
or other favorite recipe

1 (16-oz.) pkg. mozzarella
cheese, shredded

½ cup grated Parmesan cheese

½ tsp. fresh basil

Istruzioni:

Cover a cookie sheet with paper towels. Slice eggplant into ½-inch slices and place on the paper towels.

Lightly salt the eggplant slices and let stand for 30 minutes.

Remove eggplant from the cookie sheet and run under cold water. Pat dry. Preheat oven to 350 degrees. Dip eggplant slices in egg, then in flour. Place in a single layer in a lightly oiled sauté pan. Brown for 5 minutes on each side. Place cooked slices on a paper towel to cool.

When all the slices have been sautéed, spread pasta sauce in a 9x13 baking dish to cover the bottom. Place a layer of eggplant slices in the sauce. Sprinkle with mozzarella and Parmesan cheeses.

Repeat with remaining ingredients, ending with the cheeses.

Sprinkle basil on top. Bake in preheated oven for 35 minutes, or until golden brown.

A tavola non si invecchia.
(Translation: You don't age while seated for an Italian meal.)

Uncle Dale's
Eggplant Parmesan

92

Heidi's Chicken Parmesan Bake ✳✳✳✳✳✳✳

Makes **6–8** *Servings*

Ingredienti:

1 cup butter

1 cup seasoned breadcrumbs

¾ cup freshly grated Parmesan cheese, plus more for the final topping.

1–2 cloves garlic, minced

1 tsp. dried basil

1/2 tsp. salt

1/2 tsp. pepper

6–8 boneless, skinless chicken breasts

marinara sauce

Istruzioni:

Preheat oven to 350 degrees. Line a 9 x 13 casserole pan with parchment paper. Set aside. Melt butter, and set aside.

In a medium bowl, combine breadcrumbs, grated cheese, garlic, and seasonings. Toss all together until evenly distributed. Dip chicken in melted butter, then dip immediately into breadcrumb mixture, coating both sides of the chicken. Place chicken into prepared casserole pan. Bake for 50–55 minutes, or until golden brown and thoroughly cooked, but not dry.

Remove from oven and spoon about 2–3 tablespoons of marinara sauce over each breast. Sprinkle more Parmesan cheese (liberally) over each individual chicken breast. Return to oven for 3–5 minutes until cheese melts. Remove from oven and let stand 3–5 minutes or so. Serve.

This entrée is nice with fettuccini and a green salad.

✳ ✳ ✳ ✳ ✳ ✳ ✳ ✳ ✳ ✳ ✳ ✳ ✳ ✳ ✳ ✳ ✳

Most Italians have relatives named either Joe or Mary.

Our Favorite Saturday Night Pizza ✳✳✳✳

Makes Two **8"** Pizzas

Ingredienti:

1 (17-oz.) ball of pizza dough, either homemade—
  see the "Perfection Pizza Dough" recipe
  (see page 33)—or store-bought

2 Roma tomatoes

Parmesan cheese

6–8 fresh basil leaves, sliced in half

1–2 cups of marinara/pizza sauce

8 oz. fresh mozzarella, sliced in round pieces

10 olives (I like to use kalamata olives), sliced

Istruzioni:

Divide dough in two balls. Roll out each section of dough on a floured surface, making 2 eight-inch pizza crusts. Cover each crust with sauce. Top with tomatoes, slices of mozzarella, basil leaves, and olives. When fresh out of the oven, sprinkle with Parmesan cheese.

If using a pizza pan: Bake at 400 degrees for 15–20 minutes.

If using a pizza stone (my preference): Rub pizza stone with olive oil and bake in a 500 degree oven for an hour before baking pizza. Follow directions above, assembling pizza on stone. Bake for 8–10 minutes.

✳ ✳ ✳ ✳ ✳ ✳ ✳ ✳ ✳ ✳ ✳ ✳ ✳ ✳ ✳ ✳ ✳ ✳ ✳

You can always tell when Mama had leftovers in the fridge that were about to expire – because they would all end up on the pizza we had for dinner.

Famoso Famiglia Roast

✳ ✳ ✳ ✳ ✳ ✳ ✳ ✳ ✳ ✳ ✳ ✳ ✳ ✳ ✳ ✳ ✳ ✳ ✳ ✳

Makes
4–6
Servings

Ingredienti:

1 Tbsp. bacon drippings

1 Tbsp. olive oil

2 cloves fresh garlic, chopped

2 lbs. bottom/rump roast

3 large potatoes, washed, scrubbed, and chunked

2 large carrots, scrubbed and
chunked (cut on the diagonal)

1 small onion, chopped

salt and pepper to taste

1 Tbsp. Worcestershire sauce

Istruzioni:

Preheat oven to 325.

In an iron skillet over medium-high heat, heat bacon drippings and olive oil. Add chopped garlic. Brown all sides of the roast, just searing them, to seal in the juices. Place roast, drippings, and garlic into prepared (sprayed) large casserole dish with lid. Add potatoes, carrots, and onion, then salt and pepper. Drizzle the Worcestershire sauce over the roast. Cover and bake for about 3 hours. Baste twice.

Note: This recipe can be cooked in a large slow-cooker. Follow the instructions above and cook on low setting for 8 hours, or until meat just falls apart with a fork.

✳ ✳ ✳ ✳ ✳ ✳ ✳ ✳ ✳ ✳ ✳ ✳ ✳ ✳ ✳ ✳ ✳ ✳ ✳ ✳

When Italian families act out the Nativity scene every Christmas, the
kids fight over who gets to be one of the three "wise guys."

Italian Quiche

Makes **6** *Servings*

Ingredienti:

2 Roma tomatoes, chopped

⅔ cup chopped mushrooms

1 Tbsp. red onion, chopped

¾ cup applewood-smoked ham, sliced

3–4 basil leaves, coarsely chopped

½ cup grated mozzarella cheese

2 tsp. of oregano

1 Tbsp. Parmesan cheese

7 eggs

3 Tbsp. milk

salt and pepper to taste

1 pie crust (not cooked)

Istruzioni:

Preheat oven to 350 degrees. In large bowl, combine tomatoes, mushrooms, red onion, ham, basil, mozzarella, oregano, and Parmesan. Stir until all ingredients are mixed. In a separate bowl, whisk together eggs, milk, salt, and pepper. Add egg mixture to the rest of the ingredients. Stir. Pour into pie crust. Bake for 25–30 minutes, or until pie crust is golden brown.

Friends would always want to hang out at my house after school to do homework because they knew that they would get a meal—or two—from my Italian mother during study time.

Linguine with Clam Sauce

✳ ✳ ✳ ✳ ✳ ✳ ✳ ✳ ✳ ✳ ✳ ✳ ✳ ✳ ✳ ✳ ✳ ✳ ✳

Makes
6
Servings

Ingredienti:

3 Tbsp. butter

3 Tbsp. olive oil

2 tsp. garlic, finely chopped

1/8 tsp. white pepper

¼ tsp. salt

1 Tbsp. dried parsley

5 Tbsp. flour

1 cup clam juice

¼ cup vegetable broth

1 (10-oz.) can whole baby clams, with juice reserved

1 (6.5-oz.) can of chopped clams, with juice reserved

2 Tbsp. half-and-half

1 lb. linguine, cooked according to
   package directions

Parmesan cheese, for serving

Istruzioni:

In a large skillet, melt the butter and olive oil on medium-low heat. Add the chopped garlic, white pepper, salt, and dried parsley. Cook for 5 minutes, stirring often, until the garlic is soft. Add in the flour to form a roux. Cook for an additional 2 minutes. Next, add in the clam juice reserved from the canned clams, the additional clam juice, and the broth. Bring to a low boil and add the canned clams. Turn the heat to low and add the half-and-half. Cover and let it sit on the stove, on the lowest temperature, for about 30 minutes, so all the flavors have time to marry. Toss with spaghetti and top with Parmesan cheese.

✳ ✳ ✳ ✳ ✳ ✳ ✳ ✳ ✳ ✳ ✳ ✳ ✳ ✳ ✳ ✳ ✳ ✳ ✳

From my niece Jenny:
"This recipe is my version of a family favorite from a local restaurant.
My dear uncle, who passed away far too early in life, enjoyed this dish.
It was one of the only things he said he could stomach during his fight with cancer.
Every time we eat it, we always think of Uncle Larry and his big smile."

Italian Roast Beef Sandwich

✳ ✳ ✳ ✳ ✳ ✳ ✳ ✳

Makes
1
Sandwich

Ingredienti (per sandwich):

2 slices thick white bread

2 slices mozzarella cheese

1–2 pieces thinly sliced Italian roast beef

2 fresh basil leaves, roughly chopped

red onion slices to taste

1 Tbsp. sundried pesto (or regular pesto)

1 tsp. butter, for frying

Istruzioni:

Heat butter on low in a frying pan. To assemble sandwich, place cheese, roast beef, basil, and red onions on one slice of the bread. Spread the pesto on the remaining slice, and place on other half of sandwich. Fry in butter on both sides until light golden brown.

✳ ✳ ✳ ✳ ✳ ✳ ✳ ✳ ✳ ✳ ✳ ✳ ✳ ✳ ✳ ✳ ✳ ✳ ✳

Love thy neighbor as thyself. But if they share
their pasta with you, love them even more.

Chicken Primavera

Makes **4** Servings

Ingredienti:

1 egg

1 cup of Italian bread crumbs

8 oz. of your favorite marinara sauce, divided

4 medium chicken breasts, defrosted if using frozen

1 cup shredded mozzarella cheese

3 Tbsp. of Parmesan cheese

3½–4 cups cooked pasta

Istuzioni:

Preheat oven to 375 degrees. In a shallow dish, whisk egg. Dip each chicken breast in egg and then coat in bread crumbs. In a frying pan coated with cooking spray, brown chicken on each side. Pour half of the red sauce in the base of a 9x13 pan. Add cooked chicken. Top with remaining sauce and mozzarella cheese. Finish with Parmesan cheese. Cover with foil and cook for 25–30 minutes.

Place cooked chicken on a bed of pasta.

The most pressing question in any Italian household is: "When do we eat?"

Seaside Scampi

✳ ✳ ✳ ✳ ✳ ✳ ✳ ✳ ✳ ✳ ✳ ✳ ✳ ✳ ✳ ✳ ✳ ✳ ✳ ✳

Makes
6–8
Servings

Ingredienti:

½ cup butter

¼ cup olive oil

2 cloves garlic, peeled and chopped

juice of a ½ lemon

1 Tbsp. Dijon mustard

¼ cup minced fresh parsley

1 lb. shrimp, uncooked

2 Roma tomatoes, diced

Istruzioni:

Trim, rinse, and pat dry shrimp. Set aside. Melt butter in a large sauté pan. Add olive oil and garlic and sauté over medium heat. Add lemon, mustard, and parsley. Mix well. Add shrimp and cook until pink. Remove from heat. Add tomatoes right before serving. Serve over cooked pasta or rice.

✳ ✳ ✳ ✳ ✳ ✳ ✳ ✳ ✳ ✳ ✳ ✳ ✳ ✳ ✳ ✳ ✳ ✳ ✳ ✳

Most unmarried Italians live with their parents.
I put marriage off as long as I could so I could
enjoy my Mama's meatballs every Sunday.

Cousin Bill Rosa's Meatball Sub Casserole ✳ ✳ ✳ ✳ ✳ ✳ ✳ ✳ ✳

Makes
3–4
Servings

Ingredienti:

1 lb. loaf Italian, bread cut to 1-inch slices

1 (8-oz.) pkg. cream cheese, softened

½ cup mayonnaise

1 tsp. Italian seasoning

¼ tsp. pepper

2 cups shredded mozzarella cheese, divided

3–4 cups of your favorite red sauce

1 cup water

2 cloves garlic, minced

½–1 lb. cooked meatballs

Istruzioni:

Arrange bread in single layer in ungreased 9x13 baking dish. Combine cream cheese, mayonnaise, seasoning, and pepper. Spread over bread and sprinkle with ½ cup mozzarella cheese.

Combine sauce, water, and garlic. Add meatballs. Pour over bread/cheese mix. Sprinkle with remaining mozzarella cheese. Bake at 350 degrees for 30 minutes.

✳ ✳ ✳ ✳ ✳ ✳ ✳ ✳ ✳ ✳ ✳ ✳ ✳ ✳ ✳ ✳ ✳ ✳

I am sure that Italians were the ones who invented elastic waistbands.
That second helping of pasta is worth the fashion crime.

Millie's Meatballs

✳ ✳ ✳ ✳ ✳ ✳ ✳ ✳ ✳ ✳ ✳ ✳ ✳ ✳ ✳ ✳ ✳ ✳ ✳ ✳

Makes
6-8
Servings

Ingredienti:

1 egg

1 (1-oz.) envelope of dry onion soup mix

1 tsp garlic from a jar or 1–2 cloves fresh garlic, peeled and chopped

½ tsp black pepper

1½ lbs. lean ground beef (at least 93 % lean)

⅔ cup Italian seasoned bread crumbs

¾ cup evaporated milk

Istruzioni:

Preheat oven to 350. Spray a 9 x 13 baking dish with nonstick coating.

In large bowl combine well: egg, soup mix, garlic and pepper. With a fork, mix in ground beef and bread crumbs. Stir in evaporated milk. Mixture should not be too dry, but well moistened. Roll into about 24 golf ball sized meatballs and place in baking dish, making sure the meatballs do not touch each other. Cover with foil or glass lid. Bake for 28-35 minutes. These meatballs can be served alone or drenched in your favorite red , pink or sweet and sour sauce.

✳ ✳ ✳ ✳ ✳ ✳ ✳ ✳ ✳ ✳ ✳ ✳ ✳ ✳ ✳ ✳ ✳ ✳ ✳ ✳

My mother died far too young in 2008. Weeks after her death, a dear former BYU roommate of mine sent me my mother's recipe for the meatballs I had grown up on. Very few of my family's recipes were written down, so I stared at that recipe with confusion, having completely forgotten that my mother had written it down and sent it my way during my college years. Suffice it to say, no card or flowers could have comforted me as much as receiving this recipe back from my sweet friend.

Nanny's Braised Short Ribs

✳ ✳ ✳ ✳ ✳ ✳ ✳ ✳ ✳ ✳ ✳ ✳ ✳ ✳ ✳ ✳ ✳ ✳ ✳ ✳

Makes 3–4 Servings

Ingredienti:

2 lbs. short ribs

flour for dredging

1 onion, finely chopped

¼ cup vinegar

2 tsp. sugar

1 (15-oz.) can tomato sauce

1 cup water

3 Tbsp. Worcestershire sauce

1 tsp. prepared mustard

1 tsp. salt

½ cup finely chopped celery

Istruzioni:

Preheat oven to 325 degrees. Coat large baking dish with cooking spray. Set aside.

After rolling short ribs in flour, brown ribs slowly in heavy skillet turning frequently. Pour off fat as it accumulates. Place ribs in baking dish.

In separate bowl, combine remaining ingredients, mix well, and pour over ribs. Cover and simmer for 1½–2 hours, until tender.

✳ ✳ ✳ ✳ ✳ ✳ ✳ ✳ ✳ ✳ ✳ ✳ ✳ ✳ ✳ ✳ ✳ ✳ ✳ ✳

My son-in-law was at a fundraiser in California a few years ago, where the organizers offered all-you-can-eat crab. He said the hall was full of Italians. I asked him how he knew they were Italian. He said because they clapped every time food was put on the table.

SAUCES

Romeo and Juliet Pizza Sauce

✳ ✳ ✳ ✳ ✳ ✳ ✳ ✳ ✳ ✳ ✳ ✳ ✳ ✳ ✳ ✳ ✳ ✳ ✳

(Appropriately named because: You will love it, or it could be said: It is to die for.)

Makes
Enough for
1 *Family-sized*
Pizza

Ingredienti:

1 (28-oz.) can crushed tomatoes—entire can, juice included

1 generous tsp. blended Italian seasonings

1 (6-oz.) can tomato paste

1 tsp. oregano

1 Tbsp. dried chopped onion

1 Tbsp. good olive oil

½ tsp. fine sea salt

1 Tbsp. Romano cheese, grated

1 Tbsp. Parmesan cheese, grated

1 tsp. white pepper

Istruzioni:

Blend all ingredients thoroughly in large mixing bowl. Spread on prepared family-sized pizza crust (there will be some sauce left over). Freezes well. Also great to have on hand for breadstick dipping.

✳ ✳ ✳ ✳ ✳ ✳ ✳ ✳ ✳ ✳ ✳ ✳ ✳ ✳ ✳ ✳ ✳ ✳ ✳

"For you and I are past our dancing days."
—William Shakespeare, from Romeo and Juliet

Mom's Marinara Sauce

✳ ✳ ✳ ✳ ✳ ✳ ✳ ✳ ✳ ✳ ✳ ✳ ✳ ✳ ✳ ✳ ✳ ✳ ✳ ✳

Makes
6–8
Servings

Ingredienti:

equal parts: ground beef, veal, and sausage
(meat quantity depends on how meaty you
want your sauce, but I recommend ½ lb. of each)

1 onion, chopped

garlic powder to taste

salt and pepper to taste

1 (6-oz.) can tomato paste

1 (28-oz.) can tomato sauce

splash of extra virgin olive oil

5 fresh mushrooms, washed and sliced

oregano, basil, and parsley to taste

Istruzioni:

Brown meats and drain off excess fat. Add onion to meat mixture. Sauté until onion is transparent.
Season with garlic powder, salt, and pepper to taste. Add tomato paste, tomato sauce, and olive oil.
Add mushrooms, oregano, basil, and parsley. Simmer for 1 hour, stirring occasionally.

Serve with cooked spaghetti, rigatoni, ziti, or penne. This sauce is good for bread dipping. We double
the batch and freeze half for another meal. This is a fun sauce for homemade pizza too.

✳ ✳ ✳ ✳ ✳ ✳ ✳ ✳ ✳ ✳ ✳ ✳ ✳ ✳ ✳ ✳ ✳ ✳ ✳ ✳

When Mama couldn't find her pasta
strainer, she used a new pair of nylons.

Rigatoni Sauce

Makes
6
Servings

Ingredienti:

1 (28-oz.) can of whole tomatoes

¾ cup salad oil

5 stalks of celery, chopped into medium pieces
  a good-sized bunch of parsley
  (about 1/2 cup chopped)

1 tsp. salt

1 tsp. pepper

1 lb. rigatoni pasta, cooked

Istruzioni:

Put tomatoes in a 5-quart pan. Squish them with your hands or a potato masher. Add all other ingredients and bring to a boil. Turn down heat and simmer until the oil comes to the top (about 2–2½ hours).

Pour over pasta. Sprinkle with Parmesan cheese and serve. It is also good cold.

Many family members have shared this favorite sauce.
Like many Italian recipes, it is made with estimations.
From the family elders to picky teenagers, it is
always requested—and finished to the last drop.

Rigatoni Sauce

Erin's Tomato Sauce

✳ ✳ ✳ ✳ ✳ ✳ ✳ ✳ ✳ ✳ ✳ ✳ ✳ ✳ ✳ ✳ ✳ ✳ ✳

Makes
4
Cups

Ingredienti:

grape seed oil

2 cloves garlic, crushed

½ medium onion, chopped

2 Tbsp. dried oregano

2 Tbsp. dried basil

2 Tbsp. marjoram

4 cups fresh or canned chopped
tomatoes, mashed

freshly ground black pepper to taste

sea salt to taste

1 tsp. red pepper flakes, or more to taste

2 tsp. capers

olive oil, for drizzling

chiffonade of fresh basil leaves, finely sliced, for
garnish

Istruzioni:

Heat a sauté pan over medium heat and drizzle grape seed oil to coat the pan. When the oil just begins to bubble, add the garlic and onion and cook for about 5 minutes. (You may need to turn the heat down a bit to low or medium.) Add the oregano, basil, and marjoram and sauté for a couple of minutes. Then add the tomatoes, pepper, sea salt, red pepper flakes, and capers. Let it all simmer for 10–15 minutes. Add the sauce to your favorite pasta, drizzle with good olive oil, and then garnish with the basil leaves. Enjoy!

VARIATION: Substitute fresh herbs in place of dried.

✳ ✳ ✳ ✳ ✳ ✳ ✳ ✳ ✳ ✳ ✳ ✳ ✳ ✳ ✳ ✳ ✳ ✳ ✳

An Italian house is not complete without a
portrait of Frank Sinatra in the dining room.

Erin's Tomato Sauce

Kelly's Pink Sauce

✳ ✳ ✳ ✳ ✳ ✳ ✳ ✳ ✳ ✳ ✳ ✳ ✳ ✳ ✳ ✳ ✳ ✳ ✳ ✳

Makes
4 ¾
Cups

Ingredienti:

2 Tbsp. unsalted butter

8 oz. whipping cream (but don't whip it)

8 oz. sour cream

2 cups finely shredded real Parmesan cheese (don't use the stuff in the can—buy a wedge of Parmesan cheese and shred it)

12–14 leaves of fresh basil, washed and shredded

2 (14.5-oz.) cans Italian-style diced tomatoes, drained

1½ Tbsp. minced garlic (fresh always tasted better—but the kind in the jar will do fine too)

1 Tbsp. Italian seasoning

salt and pepper to taste

3 Tbsp. flour

warm cooked pasta

Istruzioni:

Melt butter in a large pot. Add whipping cream and sour cream, stirring frequently on medium heat until the sauce base is smooth. Slowly add in the Parmesan cheese. Add basil leaves, Italian style tomatoes, garlic, Italian seasonings, salt and pepper, and flour. Simmer on medium-low for 15 minutes, stirring frequently.

Toss sauce with pasta and garnish with basil leaves or extra Parmesan cheese.

From my daughter, Kelly: I created this sauce when I didn't want to use a plain white sauce, but red sauce seemed just too predicable for the dish I was making. So I made a "pink sauce"—a hybrid of delicious marinara sauce, combined with a creamy, cheesy base. I have tweaked it over the years so that it is the best of both worlds, and friends and family have liked the "out of the box" solution to pasta sauce. Enjoy!

Kelly's Pink Sauce

Perfection White Sauce

Perfection White Sauce

Makes
8
Servings

Ingredienti:

2 cups heavy cream

½ cup (1 stick) real butter—no substitutions

1–1½ cups freshly grated Parmesan cheese (if you use the pre-grated kind in bags, you will end up stirring the sauce forever because it just doesn't melt right)

1 tsp. garlic salt

freshly ground pepper to taste

extra Parmesan cheese, to sprinkle on top of each serving

fettuccini or other pasta of your choice

Istruzioni:

Melt the butter, add the cream, and then add the cheese and spices over medium heat. Stir, stir, stir. Don't cook on high or you will scorch the sauce. It takes a good 20 minutes of prep, but by the time your pasta is done, your sauce will be done as well. (Note: Don't microwave the leftover sauce. It will separate. You will need to warm it in a pan.)

Cook your pasta al-dente and serve with the sauce. Delicious with hot bread, grilled chicken, or just plain. Have a salad and your meal is complete.

To those who are "pure-blooded" Italian, this recipe is served as an appetizer. For those who don't know any better, this dish may be mistaken as the main course. My Italian mother would always say that a meal was not complete unless there was a bowl of pasta on the table, no matter what was being served for dinner.

Simple-Simple Mushroom Sauce ✳✳✳✳✳✳

Ingredienti:

1 lb. mushrooms (lower stems removed), washed well, finely sliced

2 cups heavy cream

2 cloves garlic, minced

6 leaves fresh thyme, minced

salt and pepper to taste

dash or two paprika

2 cups Parmesan cheese

2 Roma tomatoes, chopped (for garnish)

10 oz. angel hair pasta

Istruzioni:

Mix all ingredients (except cheese, tomato, and pasta) in bowl; stir well to blend. Cover and refrigerate for at least an hour; two hours is ideal for the flavors to "marry."

As you begin to cook pasta, place marinated mushroom sauce in large skillet and cook on medium until mushrooms are soft and a deeper shade of brown.

Cook and drain pasta. Toss pasta with mushroom sauce in skillet. Fold in Parmesan cheese. Warm in skillet for 3–5 minutes.

Garnish with tomatoes and a little extra salt on the top.

✳ ✳ ✳ ✳ ✳ ✳ ✳ ✳ ✳ ✳ ✳ ✳ ✳ ✳ ✳ ✳ ✳ ✳ ✳

The latest joke at our table is:
We are not Italians. We are "eat-alians."

Simple-Simple
Mushroom Sauce

Laura's Almond Pesto

Makes
3
Cups

Ingredienti:

½ cup toasted whole almonds, roughly chopped

½ tsp. kosher salt

2 garlic cloves, peeled and roughly chopped

2 cups lightly packed basil leaves

½ cup Romano cheese

¾ cup extra-virgin olive oil

Istruzioni:

In a blender or food processor, add almonds, salt, and garlic. Pulse blender a few times, being careful not to overdo it and turn the almonds into a paste too quickly. Add basil leaves and cheese. Blend and scrape down sides of blender until combined into a course paste. Through the opening in the blender lid, slowly add olive oil in a steady stream while blender runs on medium speed. Blend to desired consistency. Extra pesto can be ladled into a freezer-safe container, topped off with a little extra olive oil, and frozen to be enjoyed at a later date!

The name pesto comes from the Latin root of "pestle," which is appropriate because it is made using a few ingredients that are crushed or mixed together.

Laura's
Almond Pesto

118

Mama Gallo's Bolognese Sauce

Makes
4–6
Servings

Ingredienti:

1 carrot

1 onion

3–4 celery stalks

2 Tbsp. butter

1 lb. lean hamburger

1 (28-oz.) can of whole peeled tomatoes pureed

pinch of nutmeg

salt and pepper to taste

Istruzioni:

Dice vegetables finely and sauté with butter. Add hamburger and cook until light brown. Add tomatoes, nutmeg, and salt and pepper to taste. Cook slowly, uncovered, for 1–2 hours.

Buon Appetito!

This is an authentic recipe from Mama Gallo (Clelia Gallo) from the city of Bologna. Bologna is famous for its flavorful, filling pastas and sauces, as well as the birthplace of Bolognese. Before marrying and starting his own family, our friend, Leonard Scott Pessetto often enjoyed feasting with the Gallo's while living in Italy. This was one of his favorite sauces. He and his wife, Leslie, took a trip to Italy with their three young daughters and visited Mama Gallo. Lara, three years old at the time, especially loved the Bolognese cooked with love. After returning home to the US, this became a regular Pessetto family favorite.

DESSERTS

My
Chocolate Biscotti

My Chocolate Biscotti

Ingredienti & Istruzioni:

1 stick (½ cup) of salted butter, softened

3 eggs (beat well and set aside)

In large mixing bowl combine the following dry ingredients:

3 scant cups of flour

2 tsp. baking powder

½ tsp. baking soda

¼ tsp. fine sea salt

generous ¾ cups sugar

generous ½ cup good baking cocoa

½ cup dark chocolate chips

¼ cup dark chocolate chips (reserved for melting and drizzling at the end)

powdered sugar (optional)

Spray large cookie sheet and preheat oven to 325 degrees.

Mix softened butter and eggs together. Add butter/egg mixture to dry ingredients. The batter will seem too dry, but do not add any liquid. With clean hands, form 3 "logs" of dough. This will take a few minutes. (These logs should be about 9 inches long and 4 inches wide.) Keep logs separated on the baking sheet, about 2 inches apart.

Makes **2** dozen Biscotti

Flatten the top of each log. Bake 30 minutes and remove from oven. Let biscotti cool 10 minutes. Reduce oven temperature to 275 degrees.

Diagonally slice each log into 1-inch portions. Lay the sliced biscotti cut side down. Bake a second time for 12 minutes. (True biscotti are twice baked.) Biscotti should be moist in the middle.

This is a softer than traditional biscotti, but it can be baked longer for that true, brittle bar.

* If you prefer a drier version: turn each piece on its other side and bake 5 minutes more. Cool thoroughly.

Optional: Microwave ¼ cup dark chocolate chips. Drizzle melted chocolate sparingly over the biscotti. You can also dust sifted powdered sugar over top.

Italians think that everyone's name ends in a vowel.

Truffles Cioccolato

Ingredienti:

¾ cup butter (not margarine)

¾ cup baking cocoa

1 (14-oz) can sweetened condensed milk

1 tsp. good vanilla (real vanilla extract, not imitation)

Garnishes: More baking cocoa, powdered sugar,
chopped nuts, candy sprinkles (tiny chocolate
or mixed colors), flaked coconut, crushed
graham crackers

Istruzioni:

Melt butter in saucepan over low heat. Add cocoa and stir until smooth. Add sweetened condensed milk; cook and stir constantly until mixture is thick with a smooth, glossy appearance (3–4 minutes).

Remove from heat and stir in vanilla. Blend well. Cover and refrigerate 3–4 hours until firm.

Shape into 1-inch balls. Roll each ball in bowls of desired garnish. Place on cookie sheet lined with wax or parchment paper on tray or cookie sheet. Refrigerate again until firm (about 2 hours). Store covered in refrigerator (if you have any left over).

When Mama would send me off to girl's camp, I'd be the most popular girl in the cabin because she'd send me with a big bag of her chocolate truffles to share.

Truffles Cioccolato

Incredible Italian Hot Chocolate

Incredible Italian Hot Chocolate ✳ ✳ ✳ ✳ ✳ ✳ ✳ ✳ ✳

**Makes
4
Servings**

Ingredienti:

1½ cups half-and-half, divided

1½ tsp. cornstarch

2 Tbsp. sugar

3 oz. bittersweet chocolate
  (at least 70 percent cacao),
  finely chopped

Istruzioni:

In a small bowl, combine 3 tablespoons of the half-and-half with the cornstarch, whisking until smooth. Place the remaining half-and-half in a small saucepan over medium heat. Bring to a simmer. When the half-and-half begins to bubble around the edges, whisk in the sugar. Whisk in the cornstarch mixture until the half-and-half thickens slightly, usually less than a minute. Remove from the heat and quickly whisk in the chocolate until very smooth. Pour into small cups and top with whipped cream or marshmallows if desired.

✳ ✳ ✳ ✳ ✳ ✳ ✳ ✳ ✳ ✳ ✳ ✳ ✳ ✳ ✳ ✳ ✳ ✳ ✳ ✳

From my friend, Karen Adams: Last time we were in Italy, my long time friend and I were on a quest for hot chocolate. Her sister, an art patron, visits Italy often, and discussed with us, a hot chocolate like none other we have ever imagined. So we hunted and found the most lovely little shop that serves this hot chocolate. The cup of hot chocolate was teensy. The hot chocolate resembled warm pudding. And the pastries were delicious and little. The price was $40 each person. We didn't complain. It was wonderful!

Basilica Cookie Bars

Basilica Cookie Bars

✳ ✳ ✳ ✳ ✳ ✳ ✳ ✳ ✳ ✳ ✳ ✳ ✳ ✳ ✳ ✳ ✳ ✳ ✳ ✳

Makes
24
Bars

Ingredienti:

½ cup butter, melted

1½ cups graham cracker crumbs

1 (14-oz.) can sweetened condensed milk

8-oz. semi-sweet chocolate morsels (okay, we use a handful more!)

5 oz. of shaved coconut

1 cup chopped almonds

Istruzioni:

Preheat oven to 350 degrees (325 if using a glass dish). Pour melted butter in a 9x13 inch baking pan. Sprinkle graham cracker crumbs over butter; pour sweetened condensed milk evenly over crumbs. Top evenly with remaining ingredients in the order listed above, pressing down gently. Bake 25–30 minutes, or until lightly browned. Cool thoroughly before cutting, at least two hours. Store loosely covered at room temperature.

★This 47 year old family favorite once called for "a can" of flaked coconut.

✳ ✳ ✳ ✳ ✳ ✳ ✳ ✳ ✳ ✳ ✳ ✳ ✳ ✳ ✳ ✳ ✳ ✳ ✳ ✳

An Italian living room is filled with old wedding favors
with poofy net bows and stale almonds.
(They are too pretty to open.)

Cassata Royale

✳ ✳ ✳ ✳ ✳ ✳ ✳ ✳ ✳ ✳ ✳ ✳ ✳ ✳ ✳ ✳ ✳ ✳ ✳

Makes
6–8
Servings

Ingredienti:

1 (9x5) pound cake, homemade, box mix,
or store-bought (loaf size)

2 Fillings:

LAYER/FILLING #1:

> ½ cup seedless raspberry jam, slightly warmed in
> microwave to spread easily
>
> 1 Tbsp. finely grated orange zest
>
> ½ cup finely chopped chocolate chips

LAYER/FILLING # 2:

> 1 (8-oz.) container ricotta cheese
>
> 1 Tbsp. sugar
>
> 1 Tbsp. orange oil (purchased in the health food
> section)

CHOCOLATE GANACHE FROSTING:

1 cup cream

½ cup dark semi sweet chocolate heated on medium-
low, stir well until melted.

Instruzioni:

Cut the pound cake lengthwise,
into 3 equal slices. Set aside. Mix raspberry jam
and orange zest together in bowl. Set aside. Mix
ricotta cheese with sugar and orange oil. Set
aside. Reserve ½ cup finely chopped chocolate
chips in a separate bowl.

On the first (bottom) third of sliced cake, spread
the following:

½ of the (warmed) seedless jam with orange peel
mixture

¼ cup chopped chocolate chips

Spread with ½ of the ricotta mixture

Place middle layer of cake on the above.

Repeat with remaining jam, chocolate chips, and
ricotta mixture. Finish by placing top layer of
cake on the above.

Transfer the finished, stacked cake onto serving
dish. Frost top with ganache. Trim with beautiful
orange peel shreds, sugared cranberries, or fresh
raspberries if you have them.

✳ ✳ ✳ ✳ ✳ ✳ ✳ ✳ ✳ ✳ ✳ ✳ ✳ ✳ ✳ ✳ ✳ ✳ ✳

Mangia means "eat" in Italian.
There is no word in Italian for "full."

Walnut and Dried Cranberry Biscotti ✳✳✳✳✳✳

Makes **2** *dozen Biscotti*

Ingredienti:

3 cups flour

2½ tsp. baking powder

½ tsp. baking soda

dash of salt (okay, two dashes)

½ cup (1 stick) butter, room temperature

1 cup sugar

3 eggs

zest of one orange

1 cup walnuts, chopped

1 cup dried cranberries

Istruzioni:

Preheat oven to 325 degrees. Prepare 2 cookie sheets with cooking spray. In a large mixing bowl, combine flour, baking powder, baking soda, and salt; set aside. In a separate bowl, cream sugar and butter together. Then add eggs slowly and thoroughly blend. Combine dry and wet ingredients. Mix in orange zest, walnuts, and cranberries. Divide the mixture into 3 even sections.

On a flour-dusted surface, shape each dough section into logs, about 10 inches long. (Use some extra flour to keep your hands dry in this process as you work the dough.)

On one sprayed cookie sheet, place all three logs about two inches apart. Bake for 30 minutes. Remove from oven and reduce heat to 275 degrees. Allow biscotti to cool for 10 minutes, then slide onto cutting board. Cut each log into ½-inch slices. Arrange cut biscotti, flat side down, on both cookie sheets. Bake for another 15 minutes. Turn biscotti on opposite side and bake for 15 minutes more. Biscotti should be dry and golden brown. Allow to completely cool before serving. These are great dunked in hot chocolate!

Biscotti means "twice baked"—or to remove
all moisture, giving it a lengthy shelf life.
(Although, we have never had to worry about biscotti's shelf life
because it's always consumed the day it is made, at our house!)

Mafia Mud Bars

Mafia Mud Bars

✳ ✳ ✳ ✳ ✳ ✳ ✳ ✳ ✳ ✳ ✳ ✳ ✳ ✳ ✳ ✳ ✳ ✳ ✳

Makes
10–12
Servings

Ingredienti:

4 eggs

2 cups sugar

1 cup (2 sticks) butter

1 cup flaked coconut

1½ cups flour

⅓ cup cocoa, unsweetened

1 tsp. vanilla

3 cups chopped nuts

Istruzioni:

Preheat oven to 350 degrees. Grease a 9x13 pan and set aside. Mix all ingredients together. Pour into prepared pan. Bake for 30 minutes and let cool.

When cool, add this FROSTING:

½ cup (1 stick) butter, softened (don't microwave it; just set it out on the counter to soften)

6 Tbsp. milk

⅓ cup cocoa

4 cups (1 lb.) powdered sugar

1 tsp. vanilla

2 cups chopped nuts

With a hand mixer, blend butter, milk, cocoa, powdered sugar, and vanilla until smooth. Stir in chopped nuts by hand. Spread over top. Cut into bars when completely cooled.

✳ ✳ ✳ ✳ ✳ ✳ ✳ ✳ ✳ ✳ ✳ ✳ ✳ ✳ ✳ ✳ ✳ ✳ ✳

An Italian meal isn't just a meal—it is an experience.
Expect to be at the table at least an hour and a half.

Holy Cannoli

✳ ✳ ✳ ✳ ✳ ✳ ✳ ✳ ✳ ✳ ✳ ✳ ✳ ✳ ✳ ✳ ✳ ✳ ✳

Makes
4–6
Servings

Ingredienti:

SHELLS:

2¼ cups flour

⅔ cups shortening

¼ cup sugar

1 Tbsp. butter, softened

¾ cup water

¼ tsp. vanilla

1 egg yolk

vegetable oil for frying

a few drops of milk for sealing

FILLING:

2 cups ricotta cheese, well drained

1½ tsp. real vanilla

½–¾ cup powdered sugar

½ tsp. cinnamon

Istruzioni:

FOR SHELLS: In large bowl, cut shortening into flour. Add sugar, butter, water, vanilla, and egg yolk. Mix until dough forms, and then knead a few times to solidify the dough. Cover with plastic wrap and refrigerate for an hour.

When dough is chilled, roll as thin as possible on a lightly floured surface. Cut the dough into 4–5 inch circles (you can use a cereal bowl as a guide). Roll dough around cannoli tubes* and seal the edges with a few dabs of milk. Deep fry in vegetable oil until the dough is light brown on the entire outside circumference.

Cool tubes on a paper towels. Let cannoli dough cool completely and remove tube before stuffing with filling.

FOR FILLING: Mix ricotta cheese and vanilla. Add in powdered sugar, slowly stirring. Add cinnamon; mix. Refrigerate until ready to stuff into cannoli shells.

NOTE: *Cannoli tubes can be purchased inexpensively at a cooking store or online.*

✳ ✳ ✳ ✳ ✳ ✳ ✳ ✳ ✳ ✳ ✳ ✳ ✳ ✳ ✳ ✳ ✳ ✳ ✳

Italians attribute every illness or ailment to being hungry.

Holy Cannoli

INDEX

135

ABOUT THE AUTHOR

✳ ✳ ✳ ✳ ✳ ✳ ✳ ✳ ✳ ✳ ✳ ✳ ✳ ✳ ✳ ✳

SHANNON MCCLARY SMURTHWAITE grew up in Los Angeles, California. The oldest of three daughters, Shannon loved spending time at her Italian grandmother's side. She attended Cal State Northridge and BYU, studying art and design. She is married to Donald Smurthwaite, and they are the parents of four wonderful children. Shannon's family happily serve as her official food taste testers and share their mother's love for cooking and creating in the kitchen. She resides in Meridian, Idaho, and serves as her stake's Young Women president. She blogs at: myitalianmama.com.

✳ ✳ ✳ ✳ ✳ ✳ ✳ ✳ ✳ ✳ ✳ ✳ ✳ ✳ ✳ ✳

0 26575 11091 3